ROWING HOME

ROWING HOME

LESSONS FROM THE RIVER OF LIFE

Roman Castilleja

MYSTIC WATERS

Press

Library of Congress Control Number: 2021909377

Paperback ISBN:978-1-7338259-1-7
Hardback ISBN: 978-1-7338259-0-0
Ebook ISBN: 978-1-7338259-2-4

First printing, 2021.

Mystic Waters Press
Austin, TX

mysticwaterspress.com

To the memory of my grandmother,
Antonia Salazar Castilleja

CONTENTS

Preface XI

PART I: A LIFE THROWN OVERBOARD 1

STAGE ONE: THE RIVER 3

THE DANCE OF LIFE 5

The Yakima River 7

STAGE TWO: CHURNING WATERS 17

Five Years of Struggle 19

The Job 22

The Relationship 27

Total Submersion 37

STAGE THREE: RESURFACING 43

The Road Trip 45

Flowing with Life 54

Rowing Beyond Ego 64

The Butterfly 68

PART II: MEDITATIONS OF EARLY REFLECTION 71

THE RIVER'S MYSTERY. 73

Time Waits for No One 75

The Song of Our Destiny 79

Gnōthi Sauton/Know Thyself. 82

The Power of a Circle 86

The Choice. 91

Aligning with True Reality 97

Awareness: Journeying Beyond the Mind. 103

Misunderstanding Love. 108

A Creative Force. 111

Life's Suffering. 113

The Silent Metamorphosis 117

The Process 119

The Truth. 122

The Power of Words 124

Knowing God 125

Cada cabeza es un mundo. 129

PART III: MEDITATIONS ON RETURNING 131

CLEANSING WATERS. 133

The Homecoming. 135

The Seeker Awakens 140

Eternity and the Dimensions of Time 144

Lifting the Veil of Illusion .147

Learning to Love Yourself 150

To Reflect Like a Mirror. 152

The Act of Creating. 153

Personal Freedom. 158

Emotions as Our Guide. 160

Aliveness. 164

THE SOUL'S DREAM. 168

PART IV: MEDITATIONS OF REVEALING 171

THE BEAUTY BEYOND THE MIND. 172

An Inspiring New World 175

We Are Artists 177

Let the Water Rise. 179

Life Keeps Moving. 181

Defining Success. 184

The Art of Active Listening. 186

Changing Our World. 188

The Flow. 191

The Vineyard. 194

Stories, Myths, Fairy Tales, and Dreams. 197

The Unending Well of Love. 201

Oneness. 203

Life's Lows and Peaks 206

Self-Realization. 208

THE ROSE 210

THE STORY OF US ALL 212

Afterword. 215

THE STILLNESS 217

Bibliography. 219

PREFACE

Originally, I started writing down experiences for myself because I wanted to capture the moment. I wanted to keep some sort of record of my transition from a skeptical believer to someone who firmly believed in a higher power. Eventually, I shared my writings with a few people. The cool thing: Instead of laughing at me or accusing me of having gone crazy, I got great feedback, and some of these people even passed my work on to others.

It's been an amazing experience. I could keep writing this story until I die because it is continually unfolding. The work never really gets done.

I discovered that when you get into the flow of life, you experience happiness, bliss, joy, passion, and most of all, enthusiasm. This is how you know if you are on the right path: Your feelings are your gauge. Even if you've experienced flow only once, you can experience it again. It will build upon itself. This will be your truth, your authenticity, the true manifestation of your desire.

Just as the path to higher awareness is an unfolding

process, this book is structured in stages. In the first part of the book, I cover the experience that jolted me into reassessing my life and how the unexpected energy of that started bubbling to the surface as I dealt with different life challenges. In later sections, I provide meditations and poems on what I have learned since my near-death experience in 1997. Those reassessments occurred through deep contemplation as well as automatic writings after reading the latest studies on consciousness and hundreds of books about theology, spirituality, philosophy, psychology, and science. In addition, I have attended quite a few seminars on conscious living in recent years, including ones on the practice of mindfulness and meditation.

The initial section of meditations relates to the reflecting I did on my life after the rowing incident and a growing discomfort I was feeling; at this stage, I began to question my beliefs and who I was. The next part, with "Returning" in the title, focuses on meditations that relate to deep introspection and the beginning of immense personal growth. And in the last section of meditations, I focus on finally resolving and integrating the new concepts I had discovered and incorporated into daily life.

The meditations can be read in whatever order you like. Everyone's journey and everyone's truth are different. Ten people may read the same story, but each, because of unique life experiences, will walk away with a different understanding. That is okay because my truth is different from your truth. Each of us holds a unique perspective of this world. You have to go by what you personally feel, what resonates within. And even that can change as you grow.

I hope my story will challenge you to ask yourself big questions about life. This is the key. Because it is *only when you ask questions that you will receive your answers.* Maybe these answers will come to you through different avenues—people, books, or even a song. Most importantly, they will be your own sought-out answers. Not something handed down to you that might not serve you well.

So, if you do have deep questions, I dare you to mentally place them on your forehead right between your eyes—what people refer to as the mind's eye. Hold them there and go about your day...and see what happens.

The key is to open yourself up to something new, to challenge yourself, to expand, and to grow. To finally find your own answers instead of using those handed down to you. To be the person you were born to be.

May your internal fire burn brighter and higher!

With Peace and Love,

Settle into the silence of your being.
And let the universe whisper secrets in your ear.

—

PART I

A LIFE THROWN OVERBOARD

STAGE ONE

The River

THE DANCE OF LIFE

It was fear we finally understood
as our greatest enemy
This dark ghost holding us back
from our great creative dream
This mesmerizing dance our pulsating
heart wants to attend.

Yet we wait
Tied to our old moorings
While the wild winds lie restless
And the open crystal sea beckons.

Calling
Calling to take you to a new dream
This magnificent adventure
We call your Life.

— Roman

THE YAKIMA RIVER

You know how the deepest part of you whispers wisdom into your ear at times, but you just don't listen? That's how I was back in August of '97. I had a lot on my mind. I was starting a new job, and I wasn't sure I wanted it.

I went on the canoe trip anyway.

The warm, clear day started out innocently enough. My buddy, Danny, had offered to take me in his canoe down the Yakima River between two small agricultural communities in the Lower Yakima Valley, where I was born and raised. Situated in the eastern Washington State high desert, the lower valley offers pink cherry blossoms blooming along the lazy hillsides in the spring and the intoxicating smell of wine grapes lingering in the air by August. The snowcapped peaks of Mount Rainier and Mount Adams appear in the distance and look down regally upon this small, colorful valley.

Despite the clear morning, a sense of dread and anxiousness had hit me after I began the morning drive that Thursday over the Cascade Mountains from Seattle where

I had been living for a couple of years. The feeling had bothered me enough to pull my green SUV over in a parking area on Snoqualmie Pass as I drove east on Interstate 90. Standing in a heather-gray T-shirt and khaki cargo shorts, with the wind playing in my collar-length, black hair, I stared off into the distant shimmer of Keechelus Lake—the very source of the Yakima River. I ran through what I had experienced during the last two weeks and contemplated where this feeling might be coming from.

I don't normally stop along the way from Seattle for breaks. So, I tried to shake it off, attributing the feeling to the new job I was about to begin in a few days. I got back on the road and headed to Sunnyside for a brief visit at my grandparents' nineteenth-century farmhouse before meeting up with Danny.

The farmland was the land that my parents had brought me to as a newborn, the one place I had always called home. My grandmother was a huge part of my life and had told me during the stopover not to go because she did not have a good feeling about this canoe trip. But I was twenty-nine then and sure of myself. I had just shrugged and left, glancing at the graceful beauty of the mountains to the west as I exited the yellow farmhouse on August 7th to go meet Danny at his parents' home near Granger.

I recognized him in the driveway as I neared the house due to his thin, athletic build, a result of the work he did building houses for his dad's company. He stood an inch shorter than me at five feet nine. His sandy blond hair became clear as I drew closer. Excited about the venture ahead, we quickly waved goodbye to his folks when they stepped outside as we took off.

The Yakima River's journey begins in the Cascade Mountains, and it flows 214 miles in a southeasterly direction before it finally merges into the Columbia River. In the past, I hadn't seen many people on canoes or boats on this particular stretch of the river we were headed to, but it sounded like a good adventure anyway. And Danny said he had made the trip before. So, off we went that morning.

After dropping off my Nissan Pathfinder at a city park in Granger where we would end our trip, we hopped into Danny's Jeep Comanche pickup and left. We drove up to Zillah and parked the maroon truck near the river in a gravel lot and began unloading our stuff.

The current was running smooth and swift as we set his canoe on the edge of the clear, deep-blue river. The riverbank was full of young kids who were dunking themselves into the water on that hot day. Their occasional splashing as they jumped in could be heard in the burbling waters.

One young onlooker, who was only wearing a pair of gray swimsuit trunks too big for his thin frame, asked what we were doing. We explained we were paddling to Granger six and a half miles downstream. He looked at us strangely before jumping back into the water to join his friends.

After we loaded our gear into the green aluminum canoe, I donned the new Smith sunglasses I was proud of, and we both slipped on sun-faded orange life jackets before we slowly headed down the river. I was in the front of the canoe, with Danny taking the back seat. Once we caught the current, we picked up the pace, and I could feel the exhilaration that nature gives you when you merge with its immense raw power. For a couple of miles, the current was fun, exciting even.

The fresh, earthy smell of the river and the beauty of the surrounding trees reminded me of those summer evenings that I had experienced in my youth. That time of year when you can catch the pine and honey-sweet fragrance emanating from cottonwood trees throughout parts of the valley.

As we paddled down the river, we tried to stay as close as possible to its left bank. But then, as we turned a bend about two miles from where we began, we ended up veering into the middle of the river. Danny said he spotted something downstream after a few minutes. Up ahead lay a fallen cottonwood tree about thirty-five to forty feet in length, with a few of its branches hanging just above the water. It was directly in our path.

A little tension set in between us, and I felt the muscles in my arms and shoulders tighten up as we both tried to paddle back to the left. But the current grabbed us, and the river started aligning us with the dead tree. As we drew closer and closer, it became obvious that we weren't going to make it safely through. I felt my body tighten up even more, my heart quickening and cold sweat starting to bead off the scowl that formed on my face. That was about the time that Danny hurriedly yelled, "Jump!"

I heard his loud splash behind me and felt the canoe speed up without his weight. My awareness sharpened as I saw that I was headed straight for a thick, long branch that hung from the tree about two feet above the water.

Too late to jump, I braced for the impact and turned my 175-pound body slightly to the left, my arms up as I instinctively dropped my paddle to protect my face. The thick branch smacked the right side of my rib cage with a thud, hurtling me from the canoe into the churning water. The swift water pulled me under, and somehow, I got stuck in the thick branches under the fallen tree.

After a few seconds, the reality of the moment hit me. I was stuck underneath a fallen tree as the immense power of the water immobilized me. Death was now becoming a very real possibility.

My body was not of concern anymore.

Pretty quickly, in the heat of that moment, my awareness became more acute, and I felt myself moving into a different realm, into another place that was separate from my body. It was as if I was floating into a new, tranquil space where I felt no pain, no pressure from the water, only stillness. The feeling I was experiencing was something quite different. I was consciously able to recognize that I had entered quite the peaceful experience, almost like a dream world. After a while, I began looking back at my life through the lens of a distant outsider as if watching a personal movie of my experiences. It seemed like I was hanging in suspension, for time didn't seem to exist where I was.

I started to review life events. I vividly remember seeing my mother as she appeared to me as a boy. I recalled many different moments, including many different birthday celebrations with my family over the years on the family farm. Then I clearly saw my grandmother in her kitchen, making white flour tortillas on her old oak block using a metal pipe. She was rolling them out with the shiny silver pipe that she had brought from her original home in Texas in the late 1950s for that purpose. It was something she had done all her life, every morning, day in and day out, as far back as I could remember.

Underneath the water, I vividly replayed the conversation we had that very morning when she was rolling out tortillas and had told me not to go on this canoe trip. She had that determined look she wore when serious, her forehead furrowed and her body straightening up from its usual slouch. Looking back, it seemed to me she had been giving a warning about what was going to happen.

As my body was held underwater, and my mind remained suspended in another realm, I also considered my new job, which I had reluctantly taken and was to start a few days later. I asked myself, *Why are you taking this job if it is not what you want?* I was taking the new accounting software sales job for the money and security, not because I had a clue how to do the job or was passionate about that line of work.

I also remember thinking I was too young to die. Twenty-nine years of life didn't seem enough. Death, up to this point in my life, had always been about somebody else. Something that happened to others. Surely I was not destined to die this way, was I?

I felt like I was far away from this physical world for a long, long time, contemplating my life and death. Then at some point, I told myself, *I am not ready to leave yet. I'm not done yet. I still want to live!*

At that exact moment, a sudden swell of calm strength welled up from deep within me. And miraculously, somehow, I could feel my body again. I remember how the tremendous pressure of the water felt against me, like a brick wall bearing down. I tried to keep calm and let the force of the water move my body down the river. I actually had no choice. The water's pressure was just too much. In a way, I surrendered to the river, and instead of fighting it, I went with it.

That same force of water finally broke me free from the tree branches and moved me farther down the river. But then I ran into a second problem. I found myself stuck underneath the upturned aluminum canoe, which was weighed down by the water above and around me. One end of the sixteen-foot-long canoe had also somehow wedged itself aground on a sandbar. The heavy canoe seemed immovable. In fact, a doctor told me later that the canoe full of water likely weighed at least five hundred pounds.

I began to panic underneath the canoe, where I couldn't see the sun. I thought, *This is it. This will be my end.* I had no air left, and no end to this ordeal was in sight. I was about to start gulping water. To run out of precious air. Then, amidst all this chaos, I realized my feet were on the muddy river bottom with its smooth, rounded river rocks.

That realization was all I needed to leverage the last bit of strength left inside me, and using my legs, I forced my body to lift the canoe. I pushed the canoe up so that it tilted on its side to my right. Finally, I had escaped the water and could see the sun. I could finally take a long, deep inhale of air. I looked straight up at the blue sky, my body shaking as I struggled to gulp in air.

In my fight to remain alive, I had strained the entire left side of my body—all for one more priceless breath.

Danny's jump meant he'd missed the fallen tree completely. He was standing on the shore of a little sandbar island downstream. And that's exactly where I floated to from where I had lifted the canoe off me about fifteen feet upstream.

When I had caught my breath and settled down—collapsed actually—onto the sand, I looked up at him and saw his dazed look. All he could say in a shaky voice was "I thought you were gone, man. I thought you were gone. You were under there forever. I couldn't see you. I didn't know where you were."

There was nothing he could have done, even with his medical first responder's training. All he could do was watch and hope. The turbulent current was too strong in this particular bend of the river. Nobody could have swum into that liquid cauldron without risking their life.

Our river trip wasn't done. We were now stuck on a small sandbar in the middle of the river without our paddles. Luckily, Danny spotted one floating atop calmer water nearby and swam to retrieve it.

Once he returned, I rested briefly while Danny assessed my injuries. I had many gashes and bruises on both sides of my body; the biggest one was above my right ribs from the initial impact with the branch. It was a three-inch, open gash that still bled. The other problem was huge, blood-filled bruises (hematomas) on my right leg. Although I could barely hobble around, nothing seemed broken.

Because of the surrounding high cliffs and the distance to the nearest road, we decided to get back on the river. I really didn't want to but understood that we had no choice.

We drained all the water from the canoe and got it back upright and on the water. Silently, we climbed back in. We were both still in shock. I was so out of it and pumped full of adrenaline that I couldn't speak much or feel much beyond my body's numbness.

We had to get back to my SUV about four miles downriver, and Danny had the only oar. I relied on him to paddle as I kept thinking, *Stay calm. Keep calm.* After all I had gone through, the last thing I wanted to do was get back into that damn canoe. But slowly, defiantly, we rode that river back to my vehicle.

It took many years to make sense of that ordeal. At first, I pretended it never happened, even refusing to get medical help for a few weeks. Growing up on a family farm, you learn to get back up from scrapes and more. One of the credos I'd always heard was "A man has to work as long as he can walk."

I hadn't had much need for doctoring as a kid anyway other than one broken bone and allergies that got bad enough to necessitate a trip to the ER about once a year during hay-cutting season. Even those breathing attacks had stopped by high school. So, once again, I left things to heal on their own.

My body did finally give out, though, and I ended up in an emergency room where I started the long process toward gaining a full physical recovery. The emotional recovery took much longer.

STAGE TWO

CHURNING WATER

In my senior year of college at the University of Washington, before my parents relocated from our hometown of Sunnyside, Washington, to Texas, my thin, wiry grandfather called me into the living room of his house on the family farm. Grandpa, whose demeanor commanded any room, told me back then in 1989, "Nothing changes. This is your house whenever you need it. Your grandmother set up a room for you. Anything you need, money, or whatever...you call me."

A well-respected member of our small community, he was a throwback to an era when men wore hats to every occasion. I still remember his tepid response when, after graduation, I told him I'd be working for a corporate company. "I never worked a day in my life for another person," he said, eyes wide from disbelief. A self-made man, he'd worked since his early teens to provide for his family after losing his father to an automobile accident.

Grandpa passed away in 1991 on the farm after being gored while trying to move a bull into a new corral. His death was one of the challenges I stayed alongside my grandmother to handle. Although my choices didn't match his to the letter, I shared his entrepreneurial spirit. Soon after college, I worked for a new start-up in south Texas that failed within a couple of years. Another start-up followed in Seattle, where I sold the company's website-development capabilities for six months. That company closed down right before the canoe trip that had begun to stir up some emotional waters deep within me.

I'd never felt so alive in my life as underneath the water during my near-death ordeal. I had danced with internal freedom and had merged myself, for a brief moment, with the eternal. I had felt peaceful, even amidst total chaos. I hadn't cared about yesterday or tomorrow.

However, in my family, if you had a job, you'd better show up. So, despite major physical pain—including a bandaged gash still bleeding underneath my crisply pressed shirt—I didn't stay home. Instead, I set aside that experience and stepped back into the workaday world as a twenty-nine-year-old with things to still learn.

The Monday in August after that canoe trip, I began my new role as an account executive in downtown Seattle. I had been brought up with good values but didn't yet value myself or have a firm faith to steer my course. So, it would be another six years before I finally started to look back and understand that river experience, my brush with death.

Years of abusing alcohol and prescription pain pills came first in an attempt to cure my physical and emotional pain from my river accident. The toll of all that and of not stepping forward with faith in life included the loss of a long, intimate relationship.

THE JOB

On August 11th, 1997, I excitedly stepped into my new role as the first sales rep to pitch The Macabe Associates' accounting software directly to customers. The office occupied the third floor of an old building just a block from Pike Place Market. The location was part of the perks of working for this company, along with the renovated office and its modern décor. I was still reeling from my physical injuries as I got off the elevator that first day, but my mind was nervously preoccupied with the work ahead.

Prior to this, Macabe had mainly sold their software via resellers across the US. So, I was going to lead a new venture for the company. The vice president of sales, Brian, had mentioned when I interviewed that direct sales were risky, and they weren't sure about its success. He needed a fast learner who could work in the gray areas and take risks. It wasn't going to be an easy ride, he had warned me, and the stress level might get quite high.

Here I was, all of two weeks after my last job ended, taking another stab at being in charge of something business-wise; only this time, the biggest wild card was me. I had no understanding of how the accounting world worked yet would be pitching accounting software to mid-sized companies in the Pacific Northwest. I had to quickly familiarize myself with the functionality of our various software modules to converse with potential clients' accounting leadership.

Despite my excitement, all the details to memorize, and nerves, I still struggled to ignore the fact that I had suffered major, untreated injuries four days earlier. The pain in my leg and shoulder still throbbed, and the bruises were still fresh. The hematomas in my right leg had turned a bright red and then deep purple by that Monday, and I worked hard to try to hide a limp. The gash on the side of my ribs felt raw and still bled slightly beneath the thick bandage. Still, all this wasn't going to hinder me.

The first month found me doing well in the challenging role as I confirmed that there was indeed a big, direct market for our product. The pent-up demand kept my workdays rolling along, and I quickly immersed myself into call after call. I had become one of the busiest people in the office, which helped me ignore the physical pain.

Occasionally, I daydreamed about the peaceful space I'd entered in the river, or someone would ask about the near-death experience. I would describe how beautiful and peaceful it was. Known for my quick smile and light-hearted demeanor, I'd then quickly laugh and say something like "...but I chose to come back to this world and suffer a little more."

Lunches became rare. I was still climbing this hill of expectations, with no reprieve in sight. The stress level started increasing. I had always prided myself on doing the best job I could and told myself I wasn't about to let work demands or any physical challenges get in my way.

My body was still not right, but I just popped lots of aspirin, spent evenings putting ice bags on my left shoulder, and endured many sleepless nights.

By the end of September, things had gotten worse. Although most of the blood from the dark-purple bruises above my ankle had worked its way down to my foot, I was still limping after almost six weeks. I had a constant headache. The shoulder pain seemed to have increased, and I started noticing that I had limited mobility with it.

All of the work stress, body tension, and untreated pain reached a head one overcast fall Saturday in October when I hadn't gotten much sleep. That afternoon, I felt my entire left shoulder tighten up. A feeling of anxiety began creeping up from deep within me, and I felt my heart rate start to climb. I got up out of bed to see if I could shake it off, but it only seemed to worsen by the minute. I started to pace back and forth within the house I shared with male roommates who were out of town.

It kept getting worse. I had no idea what to do. I felt like I was about to die, and my mind kept racing with this sinking feeling of despair. *Was I having a heart attack?* I tried to sit on the couch for a moment and then walked outside to the chilly backyard. My heart rate climbed. It now felt like it was about to jump out of my chest. *This is it,* I thought. This is going to be my ending, in the most mundane way. I tried to call a friend, but with my jitters and racing mind, I couldn't seem to do it.

Finally, I came to the point where, out of fear I might be having a heart attack, I decided to call 911. I described my symptoms to the operator, and she dispatched first medical responders. I hung up and waited anxiously for them.

Within minutes I could hear sirens approaching. I ran out and met a team from the fire department in front of the house. They rushed me back inside, sat me on my couch, and started asking questions while one quickly checked my vitals. My heart rate was above 185 beats per minute. They asked, "Have you been running?" I said no. An ambulance arrived, and paramedics took over. After talking it over, they advised me to get in the back of the ambulance to head to the nearest emergency room.

And just like that, it seemed, what should have been a relaxing weekend turned into a siren-screaming ride to Swedish Medical Center in Ballard, Washington.

When I arrived in the mostly empty ER, my heart rate had finally dipped some to 176 bpm, but it was nowhere near the resting rate of 60 to 100 beats per minute. The ambulance staff moved me to a bed where two doctors hooked me up to machines. I explained what happened as they kept checking my vitals. At one point a doctor gave me medications to help me relax. I closed my eyes and felt my breath slowing. I was starting to feel miraculously better, and the doctors around me started to relax too. One told me to lay back down on the bed and take a nap if needed.

I put my head back on the pillow and started to wonder what the hell had just happened. My thoughts at this point seemed clearer, more normal. After a few minutes, a doctor approached my bedside with a chart and said, "All your vitals are normal again. We checked your heart, and we see nothing glaringly wrong. What you experienced, son," he told me, "was a panic attack."

What? I thought, and then *How?* I was in disbelief then. I see now that the panic attack was my body trying to help me move into a new chapter of life, one in which I would connect more fully with all that I was, physically and otherwise. But back then, I wasn't yet ready to listen.

THE RELATIONSHIP

I wasn't dating any woman exclusively when I started working for The Macabe Associates. As the physical effects of the river experience lingered, however, a relationship that had been casual for a while began to take center stage. I had met Michelle a year earlier, when my roommates and I held a three-day party over Labor Day weekend in September 1996. We held it in honor of Bumbershoot, an annual music and arts festival underneath Seattle's Space Needle. I was living on the west side of Queen Anne hill with five other roommates then, in a three-story, early-1900s home.

That Saturday afternoon was the first time I saw this vivacious, petite brunette with shoulder-length hair. She had stopped by as an old friend of my college buddy, Joel, while on the way to a wedding reception. I clearly remember her walking up the long flight of stairs that led to the house's front patio, overdressed for the gathering in a yellow, flowered summer dress and high heels.

I was standing out on that patio enjoying the day with

my cousin, Junior, and a few friends. As we sipped beer alongside the keg on that beautiful blue Saturday afternoon, Joel introduced us, and we conversed easily. By late in the evening, a cold breeze was coming off Puget Sound, and Michelle mentioned being cold. I immediately went to my room and brought her a flannel shirt, kissed her cheek as I handed it to her, and said, "Here you go." And that was how it all started.

Over the next year, we dated on occasion, attending movies and NBA games together. I quickly learned that, for a smaller woman, she could carry the room with her energy if she wanted to, which I really admired. Michelle also was curious and adventurous and helped expand my enjoyment of reading, listening to music, and the arts.

Right after the emergency room episode that fall, I also began to see how truly caring she was. Michelle started to come by my house more often and often checked in with me at work to see how I was doing. The panic attack had only jarred me a bit, I thought at the time, and even if I had realized how much it had thrown me, I didn't know where to begin to get help or who to share this information with. So, the following Monday morning, I went back to work as if nothing had happened.

Within a few weeks, my body rebelled, and I could barely get out of bed. I could barely move my shoulder, and the headaches became extremely debilitating. I—for the first time in a long time—called in sick. The sick days became more common in mid-November as I reached the point where I couldn't function normally, either physically or emotionally, due to lack of sleep and pain. I couldn't even drive.

Michelle came up with a plan to take me to her parents' home in Port Orchard where someone could watch over me. Her dad also had relationships with physicians there who could possibly help. So, off we went one morning, taking the West Seattle, Fauntleroy ferry to Southworth, after which she drove us to her parents' home.

Over the next two weeks, with her parents' help, I visited various doctors, including internal medicine specialists and gastroenterologists. The rounds of tests I endured finally brought two diagnoses. First, I had seriously injured the soft tissue around my shoulder; the injury by now had formed scar tissue that was limiting my shoulder mobility. I also had a pretty bad sinus issue, which would require surgery. The combination had led to the health nightmare.

To help break down the scar tissue, I would begin seeing a physical therapist back in Seattle. And an initial sinus surgery was scheduled during which a doctor planned on fixing what turned out to be a deviated septum in my nose, as well as cleaning out my sinuses. In addition, I started seeing energy healers, massage therapists, acupuncturists, naturopathic doctors, and others, trying new treatments in the hope of relief for my soft tissue and sinus issues.

Michelle and I began to get a lot closer during those

two weeks in Port Orchard. She commuted daily to her finance position at a tech start-up in Seattle via ferry but made sure to spend evenings beside me at her parents' home. It was a sign of commitment I did not take lightly.

I was lucky in other ways as well. My Seattle employer had been really understanding, partly I think because they had seen my true work ethic by that point. So, even though I had been absent for almost three weeks, they accepted it. This time, in fact, my boss hired an assistant for me as soon as I got back and added more bodies to the team soon after. It looked like I was firmly back on the saddle job-wise.

As sunny as things seemed from the outside, though, I lived in an emotional world that was becoming cloaked in darkness. After the canoe accident, I had started to drink a lot more alcohol than normal. My weekends gradually became a string of binging days where alcohol numbed me to the physical pain I was living with. I was "self-medicating," a doctor told me years later, to try to cope with the physical and mental trauma of the rowing accident.

The physicians I started seeing also began prescribing painkillers such as Vicodin, Percocet, and tramadol. To that list of drugs, muscle relaxers were added for the soft-tissue injuries and antibiotics for the regular sinus infections I now had. All kinds of different pills began accumulating in my medicine cabinet, only these drugs were doctor-approved.

My health challenges kept escalating over the following four years. I had my first sinus surgery in 1998 to fix the deviated septum. My regular doctor at that point asked me if I understood what I was in for. When I said it seemed to be a simple outpatient surgery, needing a rough couple of days of recovery, he proceeded to tell me that they were going to have to cut some cartilage and bone in my nose and reset it. Needless to say, I was not looking forward to it.

After the surgery, I fully understood why he had told me those details in such a grave voice. Once the initial surgery drugs had worn off, my head felt like it had been split open right down the middle. My supposed two-day work absence turned into a week in which I was bedridden and taking as many pain pills as possible out of necessity. Michelle took time off from her job to help with my recovery.

I could barely walk one block the first week I went back to work. Another three weeks followed in which I spent the majority of my time at Michelle's apartment to totally rebuild my stamina. After a couple more months, I felt closer to feeling normal again.

Michelle and I had by then become an official couple, and I spent most of my time at her apartment. After the surgery, though, my internal emotional barometer seemed to have reached a tipping point where I seemed to be on guard all the time. A slight anxiety permeated my days. For instance, a coworker snuck up behind my chair once and touched me as a joke. I jumped up onto my feet as if attacked, and she never did that again.

Along with dealing with stiffness and pain, I worried deep inside that I was going to have a panic attack again. I hadn't brought it up during visits to my doctors or to Michelle because it seemed pointless to do so.

Michelle always loved the finer things in life like traveling, and parties and fun were as important to her as working hard, which I appreciated. A few months after the initial surgery—and after months of weekly visits to a physical therapist—we decided I was well enough to travel. San Francisco, Las Vegas, Phoenix, Palm Springs, Los Angeles: Our list of trips started to accumulate over the next few years.

By then, I had introduced Michelle to family. A barbecue at the family farm provided a chance to introduce her to my grandmother. My parents met her during a Seattle visit in the summer of 1998. Then, during the summer of 1999, we finally decided to live together permanently.

My job had gotten easier to cope with by early 2000, partly from hiring more people for the role I had initially been hired for. An eight-hour workday had become routine, and in appreciation of my work, the VP had given me a 40-percent raise. So, I kept an intense pace up.

Only, as the years kept progressing, my body still seemed foreign to me. The thought, *Will I ever feel normal again?* lingered in my mind. I couldn't help but recollect how drastically different I felt before the accident and begrudge what I was now forced to live with.

I had started to stay out later and later on weekend nights by the summer of 2000. My after-work happy hours with coworkers on Fridays often continued past 8 p.m. I was still dealing with constant sinus infections, which meant a steady stream of Vicodin and antibiotics (because bacteria were mistakenly assumed to produce most of these infections back then). The merry-go-round of doctor visits continued and showed no signs of stopping. In fact, my sinus doctor, considered one of the best in the Pacific Northwest, told me I needed another sinus surgery.

On top of that downer, my constant use of prescription drugs had started to come with a price. I was dealing with regular stomach issues and other side effects mainly from the overuse of antibiotics. My drinking disappearances also finally started to take a toll on my relationship. Sometimes I would stroll into the apartment at four or five on a Saturday or Sunday morning, leaving Michelle constantly worried about me.

She understood the daily physical pain I had and the frustration with my body. There were bloody noses due to the sinus infections, days in which I was too physically debilitated to get out of bed due to an ailment, and occasional weekend trips ruined by a new sinus infection that meant calling a doctor and getting a prescription filled by the nearest drug store we could find.

For instance, we were staying at the historic Benson Hotel in downtown Portland one weekend when, on a Sunday morning, I woke up and could barely breathe. My heart rate started to increase, and my chest was tightening. I was so frustrated as Michelle drove me to the nearest hospital once again.

As soon as they saw me gasping for air at the ER intake area, they moved me to a room and injected Benadryl. *Here we go again*, I thought of this living nightmare. The anxiety and tightening in my chest were teetering me on the edge of another panic attack. I had done those occasional ER trips as a kid for bad allergies. But that was long ago. *How could this have come back?*

So now, on top of all of the sinus and pain drugs I had been taking, I began to use an inhaler and took Claritin. I also had to carry an EpiPen that you can puncture your skin with to inject an emergency med just in case an inflammatory episode closed down my throat so much that I was at risk of asphyxiating. I was also sent to an immunologist back in Seattle to see what I was allergic to.

The one bright spot at the time was that my job success during the dot-com boom meant I received constant calls from recruiters. In November 2000, I joined a hot start-up called Primus Knowledge Solutions that was also located in downtown Seattle. The company had gone public in July 1999 and at one point was trading at over $130 a share. Their signing bonus, plus the opportunity to sell to

Fortune 500 companies, was too enticing to pass up. Their software was also customer-service-focused, which I felt pretty excited about selling. Out of college, I had worked for Nordstrom and really understood the importance of customer service. Now I would be selling a cutting-edge customer relationship management software.

With more money than I had ever had at my disposal, I enjoyed constant trips to high-end restaurants and running up huge bar tabs that meant little to me. I was careful to mainly reserve taking prescribed pain pills for the weekends to not hinder my workdays. The drinking at night, though, had only increased. I just kept the party going through the peak of the dot-com era in March 2000 and beyond.

The weekend trips with Michelle also got more extravagant. That year, we visited Vegas for likely the fourth time, as well as resorts in Tucson, Arizona, and Cannon Beach, Oregon. It seemed like it we would be able to go on that way forever.

However, like many other Americans, I woke up to a new world the morning of September 11th, 2001. As I was getting ready for work, the office called and told me to stay home and turn on the TV. I was shocked by what had happened in general, but the trauma would soon turn personal.

The office mood after September 11th changed as our business started to slow down. The stock of our hot young start-up dramatically dropped in value to less than a dollar by the end of 2001. The bottoming out of my career came one morning in early November of that year. My boss called me into her corner office. She was crying as she told me the news that I was being laid off along with 80 percent of my team. We would continue to be paid until the end of the year, and that was it.

I recall going down the elevator, office paperwork in hand, thoughts running through my mind such as, *What am I going to tell Michelle? What is my next move?* I felt like I'd been kicked in the gut as I exited on the ground floor and walked to the new Toyota 4Runner I had recently bought. The party had ended.

TOTAL SUBMERSION

My parents were mostly absent from my life by then other than on the rare occasions I would book a trip to see them in McAllen, Texas. They both had always had good jobs. Dad had worked for the state of Washington for well over twenty years before he and my mother had retired to Texas, and my mom had a career as a quality control inspector for a large paper-manufacturing corporation. And even in a small town like Sunnyside, Washington, where I grew up, there were plenty of well-paying jobs. So, being without work all of a sudden floored me.

But by my early twenties, my grandmother had essentially become my second mom. Just as she had done throughout the doctor visits and the surgeries, she called me constantly after I got laid off just to check in. "Is there anything you need?" she would ask, letting me know that, even though grandfather had passed on, she was still there.

I took comfort then, just as I have over the years, in knowing that no matter what I did or experienced, she was on my side. Oh yes, I sometimes pushed back at the challenges of life. But whenever I got into trouble, there was Grandma, somehow bailing me out, offering support, and staying positive.

In November 2001, dealing with a new ending, I needed the rock of her moral support once again. I had Michelle as well, but our lives were complicated by the pricey lifestyle we'd grown accustomed to.

Just before I lost my job, Michelle, who had a high-profile job working for Microsoft's co-founder, Paul Allen, had decided to go along with my pouts about wanting more space at home. I was not too thrilled about the idea of house hunting after the layoff. But we went ahead and upped the financial ante. She thought a big new house would make us happier, and I somehow wanted to believe that too.

We moved into a three-story house on the top of Queen Anne hill. Our kitchen alone could have filled half of the previous apartment, but the place provided a great environment to entertain in.

I now took a daily dose of medication simply to cope with everyday life. It had become normal; anytime I felt too anxious or couldn't stand the physical pain, I would reach for something. It didn't help that it had become clear, in 2002, that it was going to be very hard to find employment related to technology, which had been hit particularly hard.

Overall, I felt hopeless and confused, and I slowly disappeared into an inner world that seemed to be getting darker. It was frustrating as I watched my savings start to dwindle, and I didn't seem to have ambition like I used to. I noticed that I couldn't even recall my dreams anymore when I awoke. Still dealing with chronic physical pain, there only seemed to be the day that the morning brought and the dark of sleep at night.

Unaware of my frustration, Michelle planned a trip to a sunny location for August. We flew down to Belize and stayed at a private resort. The stunning, white, sandy beach and the beautiful sunsets were a welcome reprieve from Seattle and its weather. During the first week, we even decided to go snorkeling. Michelle asked if I would be okay with that. I said yes. After all, Belize has some of the most beautiful coral reefs on the planet. But I hadn't been in the water since that fateful canoe accident exactly five years earlier.

To maximize the snorkeling experience that pristine day, the guide moved our boat farther and farther from land to a location in shallow aqua waters. I became tenser the farther we drifted away from land. As the guide told us, "We are here," I felt myself getting a little restless too. I recall Michelle jumping into the water first, and then I plunged in. In a heartbeat, I completely blacked out.

When I awoke in the water—I don't know how many minutes later—people were shouting at me. Telling me to come closer to the boat. I finally emerged from my confused state and realized where I was. And I did not want to be there. I hastily swam back to the boat, which seemed a long way away. Or maybe I drifted; I'm not quite sure.

The guide looked into my eyes as I came alongside the boat and hastily pulled me back into it. I quickly said I was all right when he asked, muttering something about how I didn't feel good after some jerk chicken I had eaten for lunch. I also told him I was not going to go back into the water.

The truth was, I didn't really understand what had happened. But from that point forward, I didn't want to leave our guest room, forcing Michelle to go alone to the rest of our planned daily activities. I spent most days in the room save for an occasional jaunt to the pool, drink in hand. The remaining few vacation nights were spent out with Michelle going to the island's casino or hitting up its bars. The late nights also included arguments with Michelle during which I asked, "Why are we here? This is costing us a few thousand dollars, and I'm not working."

When we got back to Seattle, things between Michelle and I soured further. My continued emotional distancing had driven a wedge between us, and I was now totally trying to avoid her. My anger inside—or fear, really—seemed to sink me deeper into despair. I felt constrained by the relationship. *I need more freedom*, I thought. And that's what I got one fateful night that October.

Once again, I had left the house to drink with some friends in the University District in Seattle. It wasn't until around one in the morning that I finally answered Michelle's umpteenth text. I told her to come and pick me up, which she dutifully did.

Once in her Volvo, I put on some music from the punk rock band Face to Face, and we quickly started to argue. We raised our voices. It was a very intense emotional fight in the car, and I brought her to tears. I wish I could take back what happened, but it was too late. I had irreparably torn our relationship.

Trust in this world is a finicky thing. It's fragile. We as human beings can only tolerate as much emotional pain from another as we ourselves are willing to endure. After that, we each have to go and save ourselves. And that's what Michelle decided to do.

Our relationship lasted only another month, right up to Thanksgiving of 2002. It was then, through mutual agreement, that we decided to let go. Our ride together had ended. No more at this point could be said.

Then one day, in January 2003, at a low point as I tried to move on from this loss, I, too, became determined to save myself. I decided to ditch the crutches of alcohol and medications and finally look back, finally face that near-death experience and unravel who I was and what I was about.

The journey didn't get easier right away, but eventually, I truly realized the one thing that we really possess. That underwater baptism had allowed me to finally fully understand something that is so simple, we tend to forget it. All we really have is right here, what's right in front of us. Being in the here and now.

This moment.

STAGE THREE

Resurfacing

THE ROAD TRIP

It was the second week in January 2003, six years since that fateful day on the Yakima River.

I was driving west along the south bank of the Columbia River on Interstate 84 through northern Oregon after leaving the family farm in Sunnyside, Washington, that morning. I was on my way to connect to Interstate 5 in Portland, Oregon. At this point in my life, I thought I had hit rock bottom.

I had been living at the farm since my relationship with Michelle had ended a month before. I had been laid off from my software sales job, and I had no place to call home. I felt lost, like I had a huge hole inside me, an emptiness within the very core of my being. Sometimes, I felt I wouldn't be able to go on living. Everything in my life seemed to be going wrong and spiraling out of my control.

With no place to be and free to do anything I wanted, I had decided to start the drive down to Texas to visit my parents and the rest of my immediate family. On a cold, drizzly Saturday morning, I prepped to head out. I was alone at home with Grandmom, and I didn't know whether I'd be sticking around on the planet much longer. I broke down in tears as we said goodbye. Pointing at my heart, I told her that if I never saw her again, I would always carry her there.

She smiled as she wiped her teary eyes with her dark blue shawl and gruffly gave me a pep talk about this trip being something I had to do. And somehow, I kept moving forward. Even through the fear of the unknown.

The month before this road trip, I had decided to move out of the house that my ex and I had shared. Within two days of deciding, I had packed up and moved everything I owned into a storage unit. Afterward, I sat in my SUV outside the storage facility at about eight o'clock. It was a typical dark, cold, rainy Pacific Northwest evening, and I had no idea what to do next. The gravity of what I had just done hit me.

With raw, intense emotions overwhelming me and no conceivable outlet, I looked skyward and shouted angrily, "Why me, God? What have I done to deserve this?" As I slumped in the car seat, a song came on the radio called "Karma Police" and slowly caught my attention. In particular, one set of Radiohead's lyrics described how somebody had lost themselves for a brief moment in time. Those words resonated within me deeply. That was exactly how I was feeling then. Like I had lost my *self* somewhere along the line. I sat in stunned silence for a bit, slowly contemplating the song and my experiences. At some point, I put the truck into drive and drove off.

I started to have many more synchronistic moments during this road trip to Texas. I got a call the day I set out from Michelle's cell phone, for instance, while approaching Eugene, Oregon. At the very moment she called, our song, "Tiny Dancer" by Elton John, came on the radio, though it was an oldie that didn't receive much rotation at the time. The timing of the song shocked both Michelle and I, and we still talk about it. Not coincidently, I suspect, I had started journaling for the first time and writing personal letters the month before the trip while I was on the farm, seriously questioning my life and where I had gone wrong. The more I wrote, the more layers of questions seemed to move to the forefront of my mind.

Though I didn't believe in what I called "mystical quacks" back then, I also started reading self-help books. In every case, I somehow was finding answers within them to the very questions I had been contemplating that day. One book, in particular, was the *Power of Now* by Eckhart Tolle. In it, the author describes an event he went through in which an intense epiphany changed his life. My biggest takeaway from this book was that we are not the mind. We are not that little voice in our heads. This new concept to me was probably the biggest idea that I had ever heard. In accepting it for myself, I finally laid the groundwork to separate myself from my thoughts about who I really was.

That practice laid a new foundation that I could start to rebuild my life upon.

The other book that was very significant to me was *The Four Agreements* by Don Miguel Ruiz. In it, he builds further on the same concept that Tolle had revealed to me: Ruiz provided a framework for how to change your life through four simple yet challenging agreements you made with yourself to obtain real internal freedom.

Through reading and other knowledge hunts when I had a break on the road, I began to feel as though the world had opened up to me and was communicating with me (I see now that was because I had opened myself up to the world, to new ways of thinking). I asked family and friends the meaning of this whole journey that we call our life. I just wanted to hear others' opinions. I had never done that before. The universe also communicated not just through songs but through conversations with strangers and other experiences. It felt very surreal and scary initially, but this guidance allowed me to keep moving forward. I now sensed somehow that I was not alone at all.

During my road trip to Texas, about seven days after leaving Sunnyside, I also had my first taste of automatic writing that provided the drafts of the meditations that make up much of this book. The first taste occurred at— of all places—a Kinko's in Stockton, California. It scared the hell out of me. I was typing an email to a friend when all of a sudden, my fingers started to write at a furious pace without me thinking. As if I were in some hypnotic trance. I seemed to mentally be detached from the things I was doing. My fingers were typing furiously away while my eyes looked out a window at the parking lot. And the words were so haunting, as if another part of me was reminding me of things that I had been through, things that had happened long ago and that I'd never really thought twice about. A new voice within me broke out.

It wasn't an easy thing to deal with, and part of me thought I'd gone mad. But I hung in there to see what life would bring next.

Starting to experience automatic writings wasn't the most significant moment of this trip as another one that happened in Las Vegas still leaves me astounded. It occurred ten days in after my father flew to meet me in the San Francisco Bay area. Even though we'd crossed swords regularly when I was younger, I had called and invited him to join me on the remainder of my journey to Texas, knowing his gift for communicating and love for the road. Halfway through my trip, I still had a lot on my mind. Luckily, he was happy to accept my offer.

After picking him up at the Oakland Airport in my SUV, we headed south and ended up along scenic Highway 101 before heading east and stopping in Las Vegas. The highway views were mesmerizing, with towering seaside cliffs of jagged rocks all set against a backdrop of miles and miles of ocean blue. At one point right outside Big

Sur, we pulled my truck over to the side of the road to enjoy the scenery from a cliff overlooking a beach. The Pacific Ocean seemed to have this mystical, free rhythm to it. The sunlight created myriad colors that danced on the water's surface, colors that reflected off the water like tiny diamonds.

I realize now that in that moment, a sense began to stir within me of life's expansiveness. Of really following what my soul wanted. *But was life still worth it?* I wondered at the time, unsure there was anything worth moving on for.

I kept these thoughts to myself as we hit the road again and spent the night in LA. Then we cut across the Mojave Desert before checking in to the Paris Hotel on the Vegas Strip. It was in the middle of this dry, desolate landscape that I had another life-changing experience, only at a deeper level than the one I had in the river. During our second night in town, my dad and I got into a deep philosophical discussion over dinner in one of the hotel's restaurants. For a month, I had questioned everything about my life. I had done everything that I thought I was supposed to do: Gone to a good university and gotten my degree. I had worked hard to get a great job and plenty of money. My life for a time included weekly meals at high-end restaurants, a nice house in a great neighborhood near downtown Seattle, and brand-new cars. I was living the American dream—or so I thought, until everything seemed to crumble away.

During our discussion, I came to a simple, profound realization. I remember saying, "God helps those who help themselves." My point was that *we* need to do this. No one else can help us. The process starts within us.

My previous view of the world had been one of waiting for something to save me. Or awaken me. I finally realized that evening that I was the one who had to take the first step.

Well, something must have clicked because after dinner, I went out alone to play blackjack. I ended up sitting at a table in the Bellagio Hotel, playing cards with an MIT math professor on my left, and on my right, a young car salesman from LA who didn't mind being about $30,000 in the hole. In between hands, though, I was still considering the dinner conversation with my dad.

Around midnight, I finally left the table and sat down at one of the hotel bars. A Jack and Coke in hand, I lit up a Romeo y Julieta cigar and was pondering that God statement alone when something happened within me. A feeling of warmth and certainty that everything was going to be all right filled me. I felt a glow starting to flower and spread inside me. The best way to describe the feeling is bliss and a little awe. I had never felt anything so serene before. The black hole of fear I'd carried for a very long time within me had disappeared. It was one of the most intoxicating experiences I have had, and it led me to give up drinking for the next two years.

Apparently, it affected me outside as well. In fact, people actually stopped me on the Vegas Strip as I walked back to the Paris Hotel, asking why I looked so happy. My bliss seemed to be beaming out from within. As I was waiting to cross a street, a couple of girls pulled up to the light in their car and smiled at me through the open window. The one closest to me turned to her friend who was driving and even said I must be smiling because of a woman.

I couldn't say much more than "no," as what I felt was hard to describe. The word "ineffable" comes to mind. As I continued reading many books, I came across an explanation while reading *Communion with God* by Neale Donald Walsch. In it, he writes that "an indescribable bliss, an elegant ecstasy, will envelop you. You will feel merged with love, one with all. And you will never be satisfied with anything less."

After we left Las Vegas, Dad and I made our way to south Texas, where I ended up spending two years continuing my inward journey and starting my first business.

The questioning and growth were helped along by my family. My sister was studying nursing and suggested soon after I arrived that I get checked out for my deep despair and need to be "on guard" against danger all the time. My dad then put me in touch with two doctors who were brothers. Both had experienced near-fatal accidents, and one was badly disfigured facially as a result.

We met and talked about my river accident and their experiences. It was the first time I had ever talked deeply about the underwater episode, and I felt a weight lift off me just by talking to others who understood what I was going through afterward. Who understood why I had coped with it through non-productive actions. They also told me about people who went on to do amazing things after experiences like mine and others who ended up stuck like I had become.

Toward the end of the conversation, one of them asked point-blank about the canoe accident. "So, Roman, was it the best or worst incident that ever happened to you?" I thought about that for a long time, feeling a shift inside me as I sputtered out, "Damn! It was the best thing that ever happened to me. I got to experience something that few people will ever get to. I'm alive. I'm still breathing. I'm still here!"

What had begun as a hurried getaway from the West Coast had turned into something else. Little did I know that I was tearing down all that I had identified with to rebuild this thing we call life.

FLOWING WITH LIFE

And so for the first time in my life perhaps, I took the lamp and, leaving the zone of everyday occupations and relationships where everything seems clear, I went down into my inmost self, to the deepest abyss whence I feel dimly that my power of action emanates...I found a bottomless abyss at my feet, and out of it comes—arising I know not from where—the current which I dare to call my life.

—TEILHARD DE CHARDIN

By 2004, my search for new knowledge had begun in earnest. Life had not felt the same ever since my near-death experience eight years earlier. But after years of pretending that experience had never happened, I began deeply questioning reality and my personal beliefs to try to understand what I had experienced. The only way I thought I could find answers was through books. That was why, for the first time in my life, I spent my time in Texas delving into books on psychology, sociology, theology, self-help, and so-called New Age philosophies.

My brief moment under the water reminded me of the famous Greek story "The Allegory of the Cave," which I read in Plato's *The Republic*. This story is about a world where people had been chained inside a cave. Shackled to the floor since birth, they could only see the one wall of the cave that was directly in front of them. Yet behind them and up above was a light, a fire that burned and created the forms and shadows they perceived as real on the only wall they could see. These forms turned out to be nothing more than puppets being manipulated by human hands.

In Plato's story, one man breaks his shackles and turns around to finally see the truth for himself. And after realizing the forms aren't real, he turns around to tell the rest of the men he had been chained with something like, "You guys... You know what? What we have been seeing is not really true. What I see is a great fire burning and someone using puppets to make forms and shadows on the wall. The fire is the light that casts these shadows and forms. This is the truth!" And do you know what all the chained men said? "You're crazy, you've gone mad, we know what reality really is, it's right there in front of us, on this wall."

What they saw were only shadows and forms that their minds turned into figures. Just a trick of light using a fire that provided the form for these figures.

Plato's awesome story rings with deep truth. We often do not want to hear the truth because it's a struggle to accept it at first. I know I couldn't describe my first taste in the river of experiencing the light. It was too deep to comprehend. The veil had been lifted, and I got to take a peek at what lies behind. That experience was enough to leave a deep yearning to return to what I'd experienced, to revisit being completely in tune with Life, enough to force me to look at this world through a new set of eyes.

Many books will tell you about this new viewpoint, but few describe the actual experience of Oneness. Authors such as Dr. Richard Maurice Bucke do describe their awakenings, and the results seem to mirror mine.

In reading books such as Bucke's *Cosmic Consciousness*, I noticed some highlight a transitional stage some people have to go through. A stage they call the dark night of the soul, during which your previous reality crumbles into pieces and a new reality begins. My personal dark night followed the first night of my 2003 Texas road trip at a Best Western hotel just north of Stockton, California.

That night, as I lay in the king-sized bed, my mind boiled over with thoughts of why I was going through these hard times. The room had only one uncomfortable wooden chair in that bland, tan-themed color scheme typical for a mid-priced, corporate-owned hotel. The room felt drab and soulless as I heard the constant murmur of cars rushing along outside on Interstate 5.

I couldn't sleep through all the chatter in my mind. I was restless, anxious, trying different positions on the bed. Finally, I turned on the lamp next to the headboard and opened a gift card Michelle had given me before I left on the trip.

On the outside of the card, a quote about happiness by Alfred D. Souza was written. I couldn't stop reading the words about finding happiness in the everyday journey of our lives. This resonated deeply within me. I kept contemplating the meaning of these words and asking, *How does this relate to me?*

I spent the entire night staring at that card. Meanwhile, my internal thoughts had begun to grow conflicted. If there was a hell, that night, I felt like I was there. The most haunting line was the very last: "Time waits for no one." It was that last line that pushed me through.

It was one of the most intense moments of my life. I thought death was once again upon me. It wasn't till later, after reading various books, that the experience made sense to me. My personal dark night of the soul happened in a motel room when I came face to face with my ego. That little voice in my head. I was crossing a threshold in which the meaning I had given to my old life was now starting to disintegrate, and I was moving into something much deeper. I was starting to question my personal beliefs. I was now traversing the unknown, my personal unknown, and my ego was having a big issue with that.

But, *wow,* was it liberating. The "now" was something tangible I could work with, a new foundation that I could rebuild on.

I had studied the Bible, and the story of Adam and Eve and the Tree of Knowledge reminded me of the dark night of the soul. This biblical story was reiterated often in many books I had begun reading but was told from a different perspective than what I had previously learned. I had taken this story literally, as most of us do, because that's what I was taught as a child while attending church and catechism classes.

I now perceived the Adam and Eve story as more of an allegory to denote the fall of man. The more I contemplated this interpretation of the story, the more it started to make sense to me. There were two trees in the Garden of Eden: the Tree of Life and the Tree of Knowledge. The Tree of Knowledge had the serpent, the one that God told Adam and Eve to avoid. My question had always been, "Why is knowledge so bad?" I had previously thought all knowledge was good. But there is bad knowledge—at least, that is how I now understand it.

From that perspective, the Tree of Knowledge represents the ego, or false knowledge. The knowledge we learned while growing up. Taking a bite of its forbidden fruit causes us to lose awareness of who we really are. Thus, the falling asleep in the fable.

According to psychology and social/emotional development theories, as we age, we gain knowledge from our parents and teachers and anyone we meet. They teach us what they were taught as they were growing up. They were told what was good and what was bad and what they should be and how they should act. Sometimes, they hand this knowledge onto us. Among other things, we learn how to love, hate, judge, and be angry by watching other people. So, some of the knowledge, such as in regards to love, that we learned growing up is good for us when it aligns with our own personal truth.

But have you ever seen a hateful newborn? Or a fearful one? There is no such thing because we learn some emotions from experience. And we may be falsely taught what love is, or maybe no one tells us what it is. We are told, "Please do this for me, honey, and I'll love you." Or "I'm going to hit you in order to discipline you. It's for your own good."

Is this love? All it really is is emotional blackmail. Or worse yet, we are never told that we are loved either by the people who fail to do in their actions or because of their inability to express love in words. You see, real love is not supposed to hurt. But all these non-loving things are handed to us in its guise. We have little choice but to accept them until we know better. We should not blame anyone. Our teachers didn't know—they were just moving along the path in this world we all begin on, moving through this cycle of relearning old knowledge that humanity tends to repeat as new generations come into this world.

But do we have to accept these things that no longer serve us? Do we really want to carry some of these concepts with us till we die? I don't. I'd rather be like that two-year-old who runs around, laughing and playing and not holding grudges, exploring the world for all the beauty it offers right in that moment—but with the wisdom that comes with experience. Because wisdom really is knowledge in action—truthful knowledge. And this is where we as adults now can choose to focus. We can choose to break free, to use our free will and create what *we* want, not what others think we should want to do or to be.

How do we go about doing this? How can we reclaim the true authenticity we had when we came into this world?

This is where self-awareness comes in. The growth of our consciousness.

The great ones, such as Buddha and Jesus, emphasized awareness because only through awareness will you ever be able to truly grow. To me, awareness means living in the moment, being in the here and now. There is no yesterday, and there is no tomorrow. All we have is now. And only in the now will we truly find ourselves. Only in the now can we cease our self-imposed suffering. The situation we happen to be in is not the problem; it's the thoughts about the situation that cause us to suffer.

The opposite of being awake is being asleep, and according to a lot of philosophies, most of us live our lives as an illusion, a dream. We dream twenty-four hours a day. Sleepwalking through life unconsciously, unknowingly reacting to our programmed dream. We become mechanical, much like driving a car on "autopilot," not paying attention to what we're doing in the moment. That's why the first step in the process is to become aware of what you are dreaming so you can free yourself and change your dream. It involves becoming who you really are, a true artist with the ability to co-create your life.

Silence provides the space in which your awareness can awaken. Some call this prayer; others, meditation. Silence is where you find the real you.

Our lives mostly transpire according to a little voice inside our heads. Listen to what that little voice tells you. But listen from a new point of view. Do not judge the voice. Listen to it. Then look back at your life and see what has transpired, both the good and the bad. The key is to change your thoughts to align with what you want to attain, and then everything else will follow. As Lao Tzu wrote: "Watch your thoughts, they become your words; watch your words, they become your actions; watch your actions, they become your habits; watch your habits, they become your character; watch your character, it becomes your destiny."

As you increase your awareness, your thoughts will become less overpowering and clarity will arise. You will become more alert, and you can react in a more positive way. If a thought comes into your mind that makes you feel negative, you will have the power to negate the negativity. For you now know that this thought isn't you. Through mindfulness, the world will start to change.

You control your happiness. Because only you can make yourself happy. No one can hand happiness to you, give it to you, or buy it for you, not even someone who truly loves you. Knowing this is all the power you will ever need because it puts you back in the driver's seat.

Which brings me to something I spent some time pondering. Is it better to hope or to have faith? I believe that faith is much stronger because hope involves chance, while faith is complete. Faith is intent. And as Carlos Casteneda once wrote, "Intent is a force that exists in the universe...and as we beckon intent, it comes to us and sets up the path for attainment."

Faith with awareness is key, though.

Jesus mentioned in the Bible that the kingdom of heaven lies within us. He also mentioned that the truth will set you free. Now my truth is different than everyone else's. When you hear the truth that pertains to you, though, you will know because it will go directly past your mind and its false knowledge. It will resonate with who you really are: your spirit, your true self.

You already know the truth. It is inside of us. And it is eternal. No need to run and find it—it has been there all along every time you looked in the mirror. When you're ready to discover it, you will know. Because it is a silent knowledge that you were born with.

The key is to unlearn what we have been taught. To open our inner eyes and awaken. Thus, we come full circle, back home after eating the forbidden fruit. Back to the Tree of Life where love, truth, joy, creativity, and unity lie. Back to paradise.

Our kingdom.

I vividly recall, the night of my near-death experience in 1997, looking up at the stars hanging over our farm in Sunnyside. The vastness of the sky and the beauty of the stars resonated within me, marking another moment I will never forget. Maybe, just maybe, there was a reason for me to stare up at the sky that particular night. Maybe deep down, I knew that nothing is ever lost. That these stars I was looking at were a part of me as much as I was a part of them. That somehow, we were connected, beyond time, beyond reason to this point in infinity, straight from the same source.

I now understand we are a microcosm of the macrocosm, part of the whole of humanity and of everything that exists in this world. I am you, and you are me. You are the stars, the planets, the galaxy, the universe. We are like a drop of water in the ocean, a part of the whole. We are the light. And what is the light? The light is God.

But most of all, God is love. We are part of everything, and everything is a part of us. We are One.

ROWING BEYOND EGO

Walt Whitman's description of a spiritual awakening in *Leaves of Grass* is a beautiful summary of the outcome of an intense period of self-realization:

I believe in you my soul...the other I am must not abase itself to you.
And you must not be abased to the other.
Loafe with me on the grass,...loose the stop from your throat,
Not words, not music or rhyme I want,...not custom or lecture,
*   not even the best,*
Only the lull I like, the hum of your valved voice.
I mind how we lay in June, such a transparent summer morning;
You settled your head athwart my hips and gently turned over
*   upon me,*
And parted the shirt from my bosom-bone, and plunged your
*   tongue to my bare-stript heart.*
And reached till you felt my beard, and reached till you held my feet.
Swiftly arose and spread around me the peace and joy and
*   knowledge that pass all the art and argument of the earth;*
And I know that the hand of God is the elder hand of my own,

And I know the spirit of God is the eldest brother of my own,
And that all the men ever born are also my brothers,...and the
* women my sisters and lovers,*
And that a kelson of creation is love.

I hadn't understood the brilliance of this man until I deeply contemplated these words. He excelled at capturing the moment of illumination or awakening, which is the moment the soul awakens to a greater reality. He recognized there are two parts within himself, "the other I am"—his ego—and then his soul. But as you see, his quiet, "valved voice" soul made its presence known throughout his body, from his heart to his beard and feet. And with that, he felt bliss and came to know that his soul and God were synonymous, along with everyone else in this world, "my brothers...my sisters." We are all indeed One, and the foundation (or kelson) of creation is love.

Love and soul are the same thing. You *are* love for you are a soul, whether you can relate to that in any given moment. It's a matter of learning to embrace and get comfortable living from the love your soul was born to radiate.

Most seekers whose work I have read seemed to have stumbled into a spiritual awakening experience, but they often seemed to have had similar characteristics that led them to that point. I believe, though, that this process can be induced. And that is what I believe all religions at their core are trying to guide us toward. Each religion started with one man trying to describe an experience he had. For example, Mohammed, Jesus Christ, and Gautama the Buddha, among others, all describe basically the same thing. The core of every major spiritual path holds the same concept. Some consider Buddhism more of a philosophy or way of life than a religion, but the intent is similar: to get you closer to your soul. To many, that also means closer to God.

What I've come to understand, too, is that it's a process. It's not only spiritual, but it's also psychological. And yes, it's even physical. It is part of everyone's spiritual evolution as humans.

Many people in the past have believed this experience happens only to special or crazy people, but it can happen to anyone. This real experience is something only you can do for yourself. I will say this, though: It isn't an easy process for some of us. It took a leap of faith and courage for me to get through it. I would even say that for some people, death would appear to be easier than going through this process.

You will have to meet your fear head-on. And at that point, most people turn back. But if you take that leap of faith and move forward into the abyss one step at a time, you will get to what I call the core of who you really are.

Each step you take makes you stronger; each level you reach builds upon itself. In the process, you also lose who you thought you were, and that isn't easy. It's like peeling back an onion one layer at a time, slowly getting closer to the core. It's a process, a journey.

A beautiful awakening into a new world.

THE BUTTERFLY

My sister and I discussed how a butterfly's metamorphosis can mirror life's journey back in January 2003: the beauty of its internal transformation, the opening of its colorful wings, the grace of its newly found gift of flight. A creature once confined to the ground becomes gifted with the ability to see the world from a new point of view.

This story, this metaphor, is about you and me. We all have the possibility of internally changing and recreating ourselves, finding a new understanding and perception of life.

I once read that Joseph Campbell, the famous mythologist, stated that he didn't believe that people were really searching for the meaning of life; rather, we want to feel alive and completely free. Most of us are brought up to believe that we are searching for happiness, but maybe we indeed are searching for more. It isn't happiness we're aiming for; instead, it's connecting deeply with the myriad of feelings we go through daily.

There is beauty in sadness. There is beauty in anger.

There is beauty in death. This is nature. This is life. The Divine.

To experience the spectrum of all these emotions is what it means to be alive. Can you imagine a life where you're stuck in one emotion? You would never know the full power of love without the experience of fear.

Give me sadness, give me joy, give me happiness. These feelings mean I'm still alive...and there is great beauty in this. You're free to experience all available emotions, but the truth is, very few of us live this way. Most of us try to run away from the so-called bad emotions, bad feelings. But at the core of these emotions, at the essence of who we are, is something we call love...the ineffable...the eternal.

Love is our natural state of being, what lies deep within you that you can never lose.

The caterpillar, the cocooned seeker, and then finally the butterfly.

It took great patience and courage for the caterpillar to sit still long enough to internally change and finally fly. So it is with us too.

Love is what transforms the caterpillar into the butterfly. Love is what sets you free. Above all else, be love!

PART II

MEDITATIONS OF EARLY REFLECTION

THE RIVER'S MYSTERY

This poem
It seems to escape me
Some seemingly lost feeling
A way of once being
Apparently lost to the heavens above.

As the winds blow and howl
And the mystery lingers in memory
We yearn for the feeling's grand return

This thing you and I call
Love.

Until the day the quest takes us
Through uncertain dark forests
Past the hazardous woods
And life finally becomes clearer
Within this mysterious river

Reflecting long enough
To realize who we really Are
The Beginning and the End

Finally grasping hold of the poem.

— Roman

TIME WAITS FOR NO ONE

For a long time it seemed to me that life was about to begin—real life. But there was always some obstacle in the way, something to be gotten through first, some unfinished business, time to still be served, a debt to be paid. Then life would begin.

—ALFRED D. SOUZA

Before I left on the road trip to Texas in 2003 I described in Part 1, someone close to me gave me a greeting card with the quote above inscribed on it.

I sat on a bed in a motel room near Interstate 5 in Stockton, California, and stared at these words for most of that night. For some reason, they started to resonate within me to a degree that it seemed like the words were haunting me. This began a very intense contemplation of what this particular set of words meant to me.

Slowly, during that night, I started to remember the things I had always wanted to do with my life.

I started to remember dreams I had as a kid. Some big ones that I did manage to fight for and accomplish even though a lot of people thought I was crazy. One of those dreams included getting a marketing degree from the University of Washington after having the audacity to tell people at age thirteen that that was what I was going to do. It was a dream that I fulfilled even in an environment in which nobody in my family had gotten a university degree and the majority of people in my little community rarely got an education past high school.

Yet there were all these other dreams that I had always talked about and pictured in my mind but had yet to accomplish, including going to work for a major corporation and someday starting my own business. In fact, I started to realize that for almost the last thirteen years of my life, I hadn't gone after any of those big dreams I had always wanted to achieve. I, for unknown reasons, had stopped dreaming. I do recall right after college succumbing to a fit of rage and giving up on a dream I had been working on. I had failed to get the corporate job I wanted after countless interviews in 1990 and being a finalist in nationwide searches a few times. I was forced to look into other modes of employment.

I had this feeling for the first time in my life that I had failed big time and deserved to wither in the chaotic winds of life. The feeling that maybe I just wasn't good enough to deserve this particular dream. The reality of it was that

I had not given myself enough time to accomplish this goal. Instead of giving myself nine months to secure a job through the university career placement center, I had only given myself three months before abandoning the dream.

Recalling this feeling years later brought up some old, buried feelings within me. And it was not a very fun experience to finally acknowledge a lot of old baggage that I was still apparently carrying. But looking back at that pivotal moment in my life, it was something that I needed to acknowledge and let go of. This epiphany indeed hit me deeply and started to break me open.

I finally came to a realization that night in the hotel room that maybe time had stopped for me. That I had dammed up part of my life and refused to let it fully flow forward as I got older. I was thirty-four years old at this particular time, and time was still moving on. Yet emotionally, I wasn't. Part of me was still stuck many years back.

A lot of us spend our time waiting for a better life to come tomorrow, waiting to get to that next level, that next step in areas such as our health, relationships, and career. The level that puts us closer to happiness, that faraway place where everyone seems to be joyous. That's the fantasy, the carrot that keeps us going. When will we finally arrive?

Most of us live for tomorrow or are stuck mulling over yesterday. We're chasing something or running away from something, even though that something may have happened long ago. Unfulfilled dreams or past moments of despair that you believe no one will ever understand. Something you thought you'd left behind ages ago.

Yet it's there, isn't it? It's there and as fresh as if it happened this morning.

We can't let go. We can't get beyond it. Most of us live that way. Still living in yesterday.

After studying the words of Souza's quote and allowing myself a silent period of reflection, I realized that I had to finally get moving again. To be brave enough to let go of that part of me that had given up or the repressed emotions that I was still holding onto. To finally let life flow again. To dream again. To dare again, despite knowing that it would involve facing failure.

It was time! Time to finally get up and move.

I was given a gift through the words on a gift card. And this gift I give to you. For maybe someday, somewhere down a lonely road, you will finally come to a stop much like I did that night and realize the truth: that there is no better time than this present moment to become happy. For happiness is a state of mind, not something to arrive at but something to experience.

Happiness is indeed the way. And life never waits.

THE SONG OF OUR DESTINY

My biggest fear is dying before I get the chance to express what I was brought onto this earth to do. Actually, I have been to that point of fear. I have felt the taste of life coming to its end. My end. What made me come back was the realization that I wasn't through yet. I still wanted more time to do what I came here, was brought here, to do.

What are we here for in general? What am I supposed to be doing? These are deep questions. Most of us have them. Yet few really take the time to search for answers and understand.

Have you ever asked yourself what your purpose is? This is the age-old question philosophy and religion have tried to answer. Some believe that this particular question is too philosophical or too hard to answer.

I believe we are all in different ways asking this same question. Deep down, we all want to know if there is more to life than going to work, raising a family, and then finally dying. There has got to be much more than that, right? And maybe there is. Just maybe.

We are all chasing something in some form or another, but what? I suggest that we're chasing our deepest selves. Life is nothing more than a personal journey to figure out who we really are.

Life, in the larger sense, realizing and re-aligning with itself, as manifested in you. Life expressing itself through you. It all comes full circle.

Too bad very few people venture into the challenging waters of self-understanding to seek what they are really after. Too bad few have the fortitude to paddle alone.

As I get older and many years away from my turning point, I realize that deep inside us, our story is already written. There is an intention, a purpose to your life waiting to be told. You are an instrument that was meant to be played, much like a seed planted in the ground is meant to grow.

There is an intention behind that seed, an invisible force helping the seed become a plant, making that seed break the ground and rise. Until someday that seed becomes a massive tree and reaches to the sky in all its glory. Saying *Yes!* to the world. Fulfilling its destiny. To me, that same invisible force is behind everything in life—even us.

I believe the soul, the purest part of ourselves, knows what it wants. It knows what it came here to do. I believe its intention is freedom, joy, and bliss. That is our song, really. A tune we came to produce.

The only thing holding it back is us.

So, dive into your deepest depths and let your song come out. And let the entire universe dance to this expression that is you!

In ancient times, the Greek words *gnōthi sauton* were chiseled into the wall of the *pronaos*, the front porch of Apollo's temple at Delphi. These words mean "know thyself."

They were written as a testament to what the Greeks believed back in the age of Socrates, Plato, and other great philosophers. How can we translate this to modern society's terms?

Have you ever heard the expression, "You need to find yourself?" It's said so often that it's become trite. But what does everybody mean by this? In some of my writings, I refer to your "true self" quite often. Most of us think we know this soul part of ourselves, know who we really are. But do you really?

I believe there are three parts to humans: the body, the soul, and the mind. The body is the instrument of the soul. The mind is that little voice you hear and who most people think they are. What in spiritual circles is referred to as our ego.

The mind is the seat of our ego, a conglomeration of

all our thoughts and behaviors that we have been taught, both those that are conscious and unconscious. Our conditioning based on a shared language and culture. Most of us identify with the mind as being the essence of who we are.

Your soul, your authentic or true self, wants to be heard. It wants to be freed, to run wild like the wind, to sing, to unleash itself and do whatever feeds its essence. What it wants ultimately is to love. To be inspired, to live with joy and without bounds.

The word "inspiration" means to be "in spirit," to be in the essence of who you really are. The word "enthusiasm" comes from the Greek word *entheos*, which means "to be filled with God." I believe the soul and God are synonymous. The soul is drawn from the vastness of God, an individuation of the greater whole. Taking a cup of water from the ocean does not change the essence of that cup of water. It is still a part of the ocean. So it is with the soul.

To me, your soul or true self is the silent space between your thoughts, the observer of your thoughts. If you haven't done this already, just ask yourself, "Who within me is listening to my thoughts?"

Pure awareness.

That is who you really are, your truth, your Oneness with everything, your touch of the infinite. Your true power.

This is why some people practice meditation. Because it starts to create a gap between your true self (soul), and your false self (fear-driven thoughts).

I have found that the first step is aligning yourself with the background that exists between your thoughts, and over time, slowly yet surely, you will make progress. This practice will increase your awareness. Awareness will get you beyond the mind and allow you to connect with your higher self. You can use meditation and mindfulness techniques to do this.

We do need the mind in order to function in our world. However, for most of us, it has become the master. It's like a wild horse leading us this way and that. In most spiritual practices, people have been told that they need to kill the ego, that this is the path to follow in order to reach the peak of self-realization, to reach that point where you finally align with your true self.

In my understanding of the optimal approach, you need to reach the point where you can finally use the mind as your servant. Where you now control the wild horse. That point where your true self that is your soul finally takes the reigns of your ego and leads the horse in the direction you want to go.

How will you know that you have reached a point at which you have found your true self? When you feel enthusiastic, inspired, blissful, and full of peace, these are the feelings of the soul. Fear does not exist here. To know thyself, to have self-realization, to be awakened—it all means the same thing.

It all boils down to finding the real you, that part of

you that has always been aligned with the divine.
That place where you finally "know thy real self."

THE POWER OF A CIRCLE

Liberated from the grip of egoism, like the moon (after the eclipse), full, ever blissful, self-luminous, one attains one's essence.

—ADHYATMA UPANISHAD

Some people believe that we are brought to this planet to suffer, and in a way, they may be right. The Hindus believe that we walk this earth asleep until we finally realize the truth, and then and only then do we truly awaken.

I believe we are all born with the basic knowledge we need to live a good life. Suffering comes if we don't journey inward to recover the true self that society helped us to bury deep.

After we are born, we are susceptible to everything around us. We are like little sponges absorbing everything. It starts with our first teachers, who, for most of us, are our parents. Just as we as adults are influenced by what we read and see, a child begins his or her journey that way too;

however, the degree of influence is much greater when we are young.

We go from wondering children with eyes wide-open to learned behaviors that are sometimes self-limiting. As we grow older, some of us realize the gift of free will. We then come to understand that we have the power to change our world. We cannot change other people. We can only inspire and hopefully somehow influence other people in a positive way.

When I was in my early twenties, I met a man who had spent twenty-five years of his life in a Texas state prison. He became a teacher of mine through what at first seemed like bad choices on my part. I had been caught speeding twice within the same month. In one case, I had been racing another car through the streets of Yakima, Washington, when several police officers pulled me over. As part of a plea bargain that my attorney secured, I agreed to attend positive behavior classes. I will never forget my first reluctant encounter with this stocky, soft-spoken man decades older than me who was covered with prison tattoos. When we met in a classroom, he brought in some books and told me, "I can sit here and teach you about these books on how to be a better person in society. But I don't think that's what you want."

He threw the books to the side of the desk and said, "I'm going to teach you about personal freedom. Something I learned the hard way while doing time in prison." He went to the chalkboard and drew a circle. He looked at me and said, "This is *you!*" Then he took the chalk and drew a bunch of other circles all around my circle. "This is everyone else," he continued. "Some of these people are going to try and make you do things, maybe try to take something from you. People want power, and they'll try to take it from you."

This, he told me, would make my circle smaller and theirs supposedly bigger. "You...don't ...want ...this!" he told me, emphasizing the point by hitting the chalk repeatedly against the chalkboard.

"What you want, Roman, is to go out and grow your circle. Then and only then will you be able to help these other circles. Focus on yourself."

If you consider your own circle, depending on your experiences, you are either shrinking or growing this circle. Some people believe their circles are incomplete and look for anything—food, sex, alcohol, drugs, material goods, money, and even other people—to complete and enhance them.

We've all heard people express sentiments like "he or she completes me," or "I need this to make me feel fulfilled and happy." The desire to fill and make our circle bigger is so strong that we can put ourselves through great torture in order to feel just a little better in the short-term. Some people even try to grow their circle by manipulating or overpowering other people through fear. They feel that the more control they have over others, the bigger their circle will become. It can be an unending struggle of wills. A fight for false power.

But somewhere along the road, you realize that these things aren't working. You're still suffering. Trying to grow our individual circle from the outside doesn't fulfill the need. We still feel empty.

If you realize that, you are halfway there. Half of how to fix a problem is awareness. The other half is action. The answer to a problem lies *within* the problem. This is true for any problem you can think of. The answer essentially begins and ends with you. You must come full circle in order to complete and then grow your own circle. Instead of perpetuating a false circle, which I would describe as the ego, you can choose to focus on growing your true circle, on owning your soul or true self.

Some of us are lucky enough to do this without realizing it. Others learn it under pressure. That former prisoner went on to tell me a story about prisoners in a war over in Asia who had been jailed in huts so small that they could barely move. For years they were kept caged. While this isolation can lead some people to suicide, he said some prisoners found something in confinement that very few find. "They found their internal freedom. They found their true self, which can only be found within yourself."

That man I will never forget, ever, for he planted seeds in me that are still growing. And for all the pain he saw and lived through, he had one helluva gift: He had the experience. He had lit his own fire, as well as mine, with his expanded circle.

Those with true circles usually attract people easily. Their authentic selves burn through. They seem more at ease in the world and at peace. The true self is essentially our soul, the essence of who we really are. That is where we must focus! That is where true powerful change lies.

It lies within. Only by looking inside can you awaken.

THE CHOICE

One thing to keep in mind: The only times you evolve, the only times you actually grow, are when you're uncomfortable. Like the first time you drove a car. Do you remember how hard that was? Remember consciously pushing the gas pedal, then making a mental note of hitting the gas, or how nervous you were about making sure you hit the right pedal? Then slowly, slowly, you became comfortable enough to drive with the radio on or while talking to people. Driving sunk into your unconscious.

If I were to ask you to describe how you drove yourself to where you are right now, you probably couldn't do it. You may recall starting the engine, but the rest...just happened. Driving became automatic.

That's how most of us live every day, not only with driving but with just about everything. Odds are that most of your day was made up of pretty much doing the same things as the day before and the day before that. They say that humans have around sixty thousand thoughts a day, and 90 percent of those are exactly the same ones we had yesterday. We all seem to cling to the security we seemingly have at present.

So, what about change, growth, expansion? Making a conscious choice to change and grow is probably one of the most important things you will ever do. It's about recognizing that your heart yearns for something more.

Questioning the status quo is so challenging, though. It may bring fear and can be extremely hard to do. For we tend to think, *What if life gets worse? I don't want more pain.* Letting go sends us into the unknown, and it can get uncomfortable. It's like jumping off a cliff without seeing what's below.

Letting go and surrendering to life also requires us to take responsibility for ourselves. And the process likely means contemplating our motives, our beliefs, and most of all, our own existence.

We want security, repetition...the familiar. Sometimes those desires make us cling to useless concepts, worn-out ideas that have not helped us move forward in life.

But the hard fact is, life has only one constant theme: change. Like nature moving through its seasons, its cycles, so do we. Look at a plant's seed. The seed, much like us, holds many possibilities. It's either going to grow into a seedling and then a full-grown plant or it will die along the way. There is no in-between. Your flame is either growing or dying.

The difference between a seed and ourselves is that we have a choice (free will). That is probably our greatest gift from the universe. We are the ones who need to induce our need to grow and finally to flower. We can make a conscious choice.

Fight life's movement forward, and you'll suffer, for misery arises when we try to cling to a past moment or focus on the future. Accept change, and you'll thrive.

Even if moving beyond the known means you see nothing—nothing except the edge and the supposed long drop down, see where it takes you. Let go of what's holding you back: A bad relationship. A bad job. The past!

Because maybe the landing after your fall will surprise you. And, just as change is life's only constant, security is an illusion. As Helen Keller once said:

"Security is mostly a superstition. It does not exist in nature, nor do the children of men as a whole experience it. Avoiding danger is no safer in the long run than outright exposure. Life is either a daring adventure or nothing. To keep our faces toward change and behave like free spirits in the presence of fate is strength undefeatable."

I understand the challenges, because one day in my early forties, I decided I needed to be more vulnerable, really put myself out there. I knew that in order to keep growing, this is what I needed to do. I needed to walk more often and farther out on that personal ledge.

Despite having already spent years contemplating what life really meant, I knew that this openness would be a different emotional level for me. I had gained a deeper understanding in the river of what death really meant. Yet there I was, many years later, saying to myself, "You need to go further, let go even more to the life you've been living to see the other possibilities."

No one likes to look like a fool. No one likes to fail. I have failed many times in my life, and I have failed big. Through those experiences, I have come to understand that the vulnerability involved gave me the opportunity to become wiser.

While success is nice, failure is where the gold really lies...if we see it for the opportunity it is. Failure can be a stepping stone to success if we allow ourselves to learn from it and keep moving forward. Failure is also a better alternative than regret over doing nothing. Having attempted something new, to me, is much better than wondering what would have happened if I had not tried to follow a dream.

So, vulnerability became my personal mantra at this point in my life. And no, I didn't always follow through on this pledge of vulnerability; however, I remained aware; so when I tripped up, I knew it. I knew that there had been an opportunity for growth and that I had failed to act. It was cool, though. Over the years, I've learned that part of maturing is not to beat yourself up for imperfections. I just try to take action the next time an opportunity comes up.

Being vulnerable has many rewards. It can really let your confidence shine through. Real confidence doesn't come from the outside, from caring what others think. It comes from being who you really are. It's about you being you. It's about you possibly messing up in front of people yet being able to keep going, not missing a beat. It's about showing your vulnerability and continuing anyway.

For one thing, the low points in life make you appreciate the high points more. And when you mess up, thus showing your vulnerability, you have also shown your humanity. People will even love you more for it because it shows what you've endured is no different than what they've suffered through.

The mindset you want to have is that of focus on the present moment. When you first learned to walk, you didn't care what the world thought of you when you fell. You just kept getting up. You kept going for it, focusing only on what you were doing in the moment. You only had one thing in mind, and that was to learn to walk. And through each fallen step, you learned what not to do, and you kept progressing. Until one day, you walked.

Failure is never really a newborn's thought; falling during the process of learning to walk is just an opportunity to get where you wanted to go.

So, it is a conscious choice to step into the realm of failure to grow. Life only moves in two directions. It's either dying or growing.

It takes action to grow. In the end, it takes getting beyond the idea of pleasing others and reorienting to pleasing you. Only then can you fully realize and express your true self. Then, you can become wise.

That is the enchantment of being vulnerable.

There will come a moment in your life when you'll be on that edge. When fear will be hinging on your every breath. Deep inside, you will know, *It's time!* Time to move on. To step off that uncertain cliff into the unknown abyss.

If you ever get to that point, let me tell you... Life will be beckoning!

It wants you to step into the unknown. It wants you to taste freedom! Life can get better for those who dare to grow. It'll get better if you choose to let it.

Happiness, joy, bliss. That's what I'm talking about. It's worth the risk.

Have you ever stopped to question and ponder what "reality" is? What is it that you perceive in this day-to-day existence? Have you ever noticed that sometimes our dreams are just as real and as vivid as what we term "real life?" Or maybe you daydream about an experience from the past or something that you foresee as happening in the future.

Sometimes those daydreams can be so strong that they conjure real emotions within us, maybe even anger or a feeling such as happiness. The power of our thoughts can create worlds that are totally disconnected from what is right in front of us.

Whether that world narrows your perspective on something that happened yesterday, something happening right now, or something you wish to happen in the future, it is not in sync with the depth of the present moment.

So, what is "real?" There are many different levels of reality or awareness. The greatest philosophers, writers, and visionaries of our time—Walt Whitman, William

Blake, Plato, Socrates, Buddha, and Mohammed, to name a few—have written or spoken about a more grounded form of reality. Their work has endured because of the weight of their words and the profound truths they conveyed about this other reality they have experienced.

During my research, I came across the book *Practical Mysticism* by Evelyn Underhill, written in 1914. Underhill uses the term "mysticism" to describe what these writers are trying to tell us. In her words: "Mysticism is the art of union with Reality. The mystic is a person who has attained that union to a greater or less degree, or who aims at and believes in such attainment."

So, what is reality? From her book on reality:

"The old story of Eyes and No-Eyes is really the story of the mystical and unmystical types. "No-Eyes" has fixed his attention on the fact that he is obliged to take a walk. For him the chief factor of existence is his own movement along the road; a movement which he intends to accomplish as efficiently and comfortably as he can. He asks not to know what lies on either side of the hedges. He ignores the caress of the wind until it threatens to remove his hat. He trudges along, steadily, diligently, avoiding the muddy pools, but oblivious of the light which they reflect. "Eyes" takes the walk too: and for him it is a perpetual revelation of beauty and wonder. The sunlight inebriates him, the winds delight him, the very effort of the journey is a joy. Magic presences throng the roadside, or cry salutations for him from the hidden fields. The rich world through which he moves lies in the foreground of his consciousness; and it gives up new secrets to him at every step. "No-Eyes," when told of his adventure, usually refuses to believe that both have gone by the same road. He fancies that his companion has been floating about in the air, or beset by agreeable hallucinations. We shall never persuade him to the contrary unless we persuade him to look for himself.

As the beautiful does not exist for the artist and poet alone—though these can find in it more poignant depths of meaning than other men—so the world of Reality exists for all; and all may participate in it, unite with it, according to the measure and to the strength and purity of their desire."

The key in achieving this feat, I have found, is to give up control, to let go and surrender to whatever we are experiencing in the moment. It's not easy, for we like to judge the moment or seek to try to control our destiny through sheer brute force.

To use the analogy of my river awakening, I was always the type of person who'd fight the river, just like everyone else does. Yet the only thing that kept me from dying was to let go and let the water take me where I needed to be.

Since that experience, I have found that the river is indeed an analogy for my life and that I can control my reactions to any experience, but I need to flow with situations. You have this power too. You have the power to transform what people are used to calling a negative experience into a positive tale of growth.

Life is full of paradoxes, and one of the biggest ones is this: If you want to take control of life, to achieve that rare freedom very few people have, you must learn to let go and surrender to experiences in life.

Have you wondered what would happen if you did that? How far the fall would be?

It has been my experience that there is no bottom. There is indeed a net, and it will catch you. Just when you think you cannot go on any longer, you just may find yourself with more energy within you than you think you had, or the universe may come along with an unexpected type of "save" at the perfect time and surprise you. It is truly a huge leap of faith, yet life will only give back as much connection as you are willing to give to it.

As Underhill mentions in her book: "Because he has surrendered himself to it, 'united' with it, the patriot knows his country, the artist knows the subject of his art, the lover his beloved, the saint his God, in a manner which is inconceivable as well as unattainable by the looker-on."

If you want it all, you have to be willing to give it all up. There is no way around this. It is what some people term a Law of Nature.

For instance, have you ever wondered, "If I plant a seed, water it, and place it under the sun, what causes it to grow?" What invisible force behind the scenes creates the miracle of a seed growing into a plant and someday into a blooming flower? And so, it is that you have the same capability as that seed: an inherent capacity to grow into something much more than what first meets the eye. For when you align yourself with this force, this source we all came from, you align yourself with the power that created everything—the stars, the mountains, the oceans, and that little flower that was once a seed.

This is one of the greatest truths and most powerful things to fathom. Because it is you, and you are it. It works through you. And it is continuously creating, continuously moving forward, never thinking about the past and only living in each moment, the only true point of creation.

By going with life's flow, you learn that there is another way of looking at the world available, and it is centered on the here and the now. Don't let your mind fool you. Learn to surrender to life, for at that point of union, you will learn to move beyond the restrictions of this dreamworld. Because what gets us in trouble is trying to control the dream. Or as Underhill puts it, you will finally connect with true reality.

That our blindness to reality has a mental component is covered in the book *Stumbling on Happiness* by Daniel Gilbert. In it, he compares this blindness to a blind spot that occurs naturally in our eyesight. In each eyeball, because of the physical limitations of the optic nerve, there is a little black circle that actually appears in the middle of our vision. Oddly, our mind is so powerful and wants to work as efficiently as possible; so, instead of viewing this world with two little black circles in our field of vision, our mind colors the black circles in. Our eyes use the area surrounding the blind spots as a guide to create intact images. Or more precisely, our mind forms these seamless images. A strange thing to learn, isn't it?

Just as our need for visual integrity is so powerful that our mind "colors in" missing visual details, we often color in or distort our perception of situations based on the backstory that our minds tell us. These stories we carry about ourselves and others may keep us from fully entering each moment.

And if the mind disguises black circles so you don't physically see them, what else is the mind preventing you from truly discovering?

AWARENESS:
JOURNEYING BEYOND THE MIND

There is a concept in Zen Buddhism that I have found over the years to be one of the toughest to grasp: the concept of "no mind." To be able to see something and experience it without judgment within that moment, which allows you to fully immerse within the experience itself, is a life-changing goal. To simply let moments happen without judging them. To let go of thoughts as they arise. Because once we slip into judgment, whether good or bad, we lose the moment. Judging requires seeing something as "other." And in doing so, you have lost a connection to it. You have let it slip away.

This concept goes against the very core of what most of us have been taught. We want to label everything we see or experience. We believe the truth is the thought label or the emotion label that we have tagged onto what we are experiencing. Yet the idea of "no mind" is worth pondering. That is the very reason meditation is such a wonderful tool to expand our awareness: It allows you to disconnect the space that exists between who you really are and what a momentary thought is.

As you grow your awareness and grow in consciousness, you realize the truth of this concept, the wisdom of its wonderful depths. For even to taste "no mind" once will allow you to experience the freedom you so desire.

Beyond the paintings of the mind, where every thought that you've had about this world has been drawn, lies this magnificent field, this space of connectedness. A world that is continually alive. Continually giving.

The present moment is the canvas, the field upon which we meticulously create everything to come and have created everything that had come before it, moment by moment. The present is indeed the splendor, the free-flowing water, the cascading movement of life.

The present is when we look upon a multi-hued sunset or a gorgeous full moon. It is there in that special moment when you look in your beloved's eyes...and, without a thought in that unexplainable silence, you two finally merge into One.

The field of "no mind" is where awareness grows. Awareness can only grow out of silence. Awareness rises out of you through the silence.

How can you know you have a thought without being able to stand away from it and observe it? You internally observe the thought as it floats by in your mind. You say to yourself, "There is a thought, and I'm watching it go by." So, my question to you is: Who is the entity witnessing the thought? This, of course, is who you really Are.

To increase awareness of your true self, practice witnessing thoughts and recognizing that you are something beyond each thought. A silent witness. As thoughts arise, you learn to become indifferent and to let go of them. You allow the moment to happen as is.

So, the key is to grow your awareness of the silent gap between your thoughts until, someday, you merge with the silence or realize that you are not your ego or your thoughts. To merge with this awareness is to awaken.

I have read that there is a point in esoteric mystery schools when the teacher feels that the seeker has reached a certain level and is finally ready for a big step. They then tell the seeker that everything they have ever been told is a complete lie. And you know what? It's true.

As part of a ritual, the esoteric mystery schools make sure you're not alone at this time. Because the structure of your whole world has collapsed; and you get lost because up to that point in life, you had understood who you are. You believed the thoughts within your mind that defined you, which society had planted.

Everything, including our name, has come from someone else. And we buy into it all. I say, "I am Roman, and I work in sales, and I am so many years old." But the truth is, that's just a cosmetic description. A label I've agreed to. It isn't my true self.

If you strip all the labels away, you come face to face with something else. You come face to face with who you really are. And that level of consciousness is possible only through awareness.

I'm sure you've heard the saying that in order to truly live, you must first die. And that saying has many meanings; however, if you keep it simple, I think it gets right to the point: that in order to truly live free, psychologically speaking, we must learn to let our past die.

For the most part, every interpretation we make about our experiences is based on something from our past. We make judgments every day, never realizing just how programmed we are.

Two people can view or experience the same exact thing, yet one person may hate what happened while the other may relish it, usually because of a different past experience or learned behavior. Depression, anger, resentments, and fear exist mainly because of our conditioning.

Whatever you place your awareness on will grow to occupy more of your focus, whether you focus on supposed good or supposed bad things. You can choose instead to focus and be absorbed in the beauty of the moment. By doing so, you may start to see things in a different way.

Our minds are usually so full of thoughts that we rarely truly enjoy what's right in front of us. Things vibrate at a higher energy level when we can focus on them—their colors become more vibrant and intense. For instance, food tastes more robust when we become mindful of what we are eating.

If we choose to pursue a Oneness perspective, our greatest inspiration and moments of creativity can come from quiet moments, from the space, or field, of silence between our thoughts.

Embrace the field, the immovable awareness. The ever-present "I," the one watching everything happen. A movement into higher states of consciousness that all the great ones have called love. As your awareness grows, so does your capacity to Love.

At its core, it's what we call peace.

MISUNDERSTANDING LOVE

"Love." Probably the most misunderstood word in the world. How many of us truly know what it is? Most look outside themselves for their salvation. For what will redeem them, what will free them—that is their ultimate goal.

Love is commonly mistaken for infatuation or a feeling of elation, a high just as good or better than a drug. And it is a drug, isn't it? We crave it. We want it. We are always looking for that next fix. Where will it come from? Who will give it to us?

And wow, do we suffer when we don't get it, when someone turns away, when they don't do what we wish them to. We suffer deeply. This causes us to close our hearts up even more.

We seem to have mistaken love for a fairy tale. Someone comes along and loves us, and we think they care for us. But sooner or later, something happens. We put conditions on that love. We say that, if that person truly loved us, they wouldn't do certain things to us. How absurd that we think that someone can give love to us.

And, really, that is unfair. Because somewhere down the line, we all do something that displeases the ones we love.

Yet we call this love.

Love, real love, what people refer to as true, unconditional love, actually begins and ends with ourself. It is rare, isn't it? Because few people really love themselves. We are always the hardest on ourselves. We may say we are too fat, too skinny, too poor to be worthy of love. We buy into societal definitions of the value of humans hook, line, and sinker.

Real unconditional love just gives—it just burns—and it extends outward. It is this radiating energy from your soul. It is a presence. It never asks for anything in return. Real love frees you and everyone else around you.

Many people in this world live in fear, which is the opposite of love, the absence of love. Where fear is present, love cannot be.

Often, we hold back. We are afraid of being open, of being vulnerable. Of looking foolish. Or of being hurt yet again. We fear the unknown. By living in fear, the only thing we end up doing is holding ourselves back. Fear keeps us in bondage, keeps us from aligning with our true self.

Freedom from fear is a fruit you reap from the realization of the true self. Through self-love, you fully honor yourself.

The truth is, though, you are already there. You are Love right now. In this moment.

You have an opportunity to turn your life around, to give yourself a gift. A gift that no one else can give you. And that is real unconditional love. To love without judgment and without fear, to truly give without asking for something in return, to truly light that fire inside you that you so desperately seek.

Because it's there, I tell you. Just look into your eyes. Look into a mirror and take a good look at yourself. You're gorgeous. You are indeed this thing we call life. Love.

Once you realize this, you will not need anyone to fill your gaps; you will never feel loneliness again. For loneliness is a farce. You are everything, the Alpha, the Omega. You are beyond your own comprehension. One day, you will come to understand that everything is One and has the same divine nature. You will have realized it for yourself. Then you will have arrived. You will have had the ultimate experience. You will smile that little smile, that contented smile, and everyone will want to know how you got it. Because you will know the truth. It's there, where we least expect it. Right in front of us the whole time. We held the key all along. The key to freedom is within.

So, live courageously. Live from the courage within your heart! And let your love saturate all your life experiences.

Love.

Let it flow.

A CREATIVE FORCE

We live in a chaotic world. Nothing feels predictable, yet if you study the turmoil, you may see patterns emerging and beauty crystalizing from these patterns. Let's take a tree, for example. If you ever look closely at one, you will notice that each branch is unique, each leaf is different. Of course, that makes each tree one of a kind. There will never be another tree like it.

Now let's look at you. You can say the same thing. You are unique. There will only be one of you in the entire history of this universe. We are all originals.

Considering what makes us unique is an interesting endeavor. In reality, I believe the creative force is a power working through us. So, what power creates us?

There has to be something behind the curtain. There has to be some intelligence behind all this. Some force continually creating. You could call this force creative intelligence, infinite intelligence, or maybe even God. The force behind everything you see. The force behind who we are. This energy, this exquisite force, we call it life. Even though we cannot see it, we know it has to be there, because without it, nothing would exist.

So, in essence, we are existence. We are nature. And nature, of course, is alive (life).

One of humankind's greatest tragedies is that we have decided we are above nature, that we can control it. It makes no sense because we are only fighting ourselves. We are fighting our own essence. We have separated ourselves from part of what we really are.

Enlightenment really is the realization that we are it. We are all of existence. We are all One. And when you know this, the veil will lift, and you will become in tune with the infinite or with what Jesus referred to as returning to the kingdom of heaven. Enlightenment is a personal thing. It's an internal thing. It is the ultimate experience of realizing that you are indeed a force, an embodiment of a creative force much greater than yourself.

LIFE'S SUFFERING

I once attended a Catholic mass where the priest spoke about suffering and why God would put us through such terrible ordeals. He used the analogy of someone trying to refine silver.

To do this, the raw material is put into an intense fire to remove impurities. "How do we know when the refining process is done?" the priest asked the congregation. His answer: "When you can see your reflection within the metal. Then you can remove it from the intense fire."

In a similar analogy, he stated, "How do we know when our suffering has ceased? When God can see a reflection of himself within you." I found it quite liberating when I first heard this. Nobody likes suffering; however, to understand that maybe there is a greater reason for it, or a different way of considering why we go through it, made me shift my understanding out of that of being a victim.

Instead, I began to understand that certain experiences had been needed for my own growth and maturity.

Following this line of thinking has led me to a new

realization: that maybe everything that has ever happened to me occurred at the perfect time. That life has led me down my own unique path in which each experience has built upon the previous ones to foster a higher level of expression. A higher level of learning, of understanding.

Reaching these higher levels is what we might call evolution.

The great Indian philosopher Krishnamurti stated that "suffering is merely that high intense clarity of thought and emotion which forces you to recognize things as they are." His philosophy of suffering was that to end sorrow, one must grow to know oneself completely. After understanding yourself, that is when sorrow and suffering ends. So, in essence, it's in letting go of our attachments and preconceived notions of what we thought should happen and just being in the moment that we can find our greatest liberation from suffering.

To me, life is perfect in its own unique way, regardless of how bad any particular situation seems. It has its own perfection, its own unfolding, its own timing. The truth of the moment is the perfect lesson we may need to learn at a particular point. Like a flower blooming perfectly in its own unique time, you can't force it. It blooms naturally, beautifully, when it's ready to let its own uniqueness, its majestic essence, shine through. Quietly under the morning sun.

The thing I've realized is that even if all hell is breaking loose, we are living the perfect lesson we need in that particular moment for our growth. Life can be your greatest teacher. The question is, are you listening?

If you doubt life's perfection, look at yourself in the mirror and tell me what you see. I see a miracle. Do your homework and find out the odds of a baby being conceived, let alone born. The odds are one hundred million to one. Everything has to be perfect: The temperature and the time had to be just right in order to create you. The odds are better of winning a state lottery than of birthing a child. You're a walking miracle. A great example of perfection.

Perfection, the way it is often referred to in life, is about an end goal or a culmination. True perfection, however, is the process of feeling fulfilled in life's movement. Life unfolds in its own unique, wise way, as a series of connected moments, an impermanent state, a state of consistent change.

Many philosophies point to suffering as the foundation of spiritual growth. Yet suffering can give your life depth. It can help you evolve into a wiser human being. You can learn from suffering, or you can revert to your old, harsh perceptions of the moment being a bad one.

The secret to ending our suffering is to learn to live in each moment. To shift our consciousness and be able to deal with the pain and sorrow we as living humans will eventually experience.

When we accept each moment as it is, whether it is a moment of happiness or suffering, we become free. We have found peace within the eternal moment of now.

THE SILENT METAMORPHOSIS

Silence! It can scare us, make us feel a bit uncomfortable, just as death can scare us. Sometimes we have to hear ourselves, hear our voice aloud to make sure that we're still here...still alive.

Yet silence brings true beauty. Silence offers the canvas in which our world gains color.

It isn't musical notes that produce a song. A song needs the silence behind the notes or between them. The blank canvas of silence. What we have been trained to call nothingness.

Life is indeed about movement. But truly, the most difficult thing to do is to sit still, like Buddha under the Bodhi Tree. Like a caterpillar sitting without motion long enough to go through the chrysalis stage in order to become a butterfly. The most difficult thing you can do is, really, nothing. To let your internal fears pop up—and for you to sit still long enough to acknowledge their presence seems like craziness. To have enough strength to sit still, to not let the fear crush you? That takes guts. It takes strength, patience, and persistence to get past the emotion of that moment.

Even if you appear to not be doing anything on the outside while staying present with the present moment, inside...damn, inside you may be facing hurricanes. The emotions can become unbearable. Can you withstand it? Can you see beyond the emotional pain?

Meditation is nothing more than merging with the silence. The space between your thoughts. They say this background, this ground of silence, is where we will find our true self. Then why are we afraid to merge with silence? To merge with the place where everything comes from? It's the source we came from, and inevitably, where we're all headed.

Your metamorphosis can only happen in this way. It must happen this way, by your internal world expanding out to your external world. It begins there, internally, within yourself. And thus, one day, in its own time, this magnificent creature emerges.

Out of love emerges the true self. With its intricate, painted wings colored by a little suffering.

No matter what we do, we cannot run away from our feelings. We can try to ignore them through food, sex, drugs, alcohol, and so on. But they will still be there, buried. The only way out, the only way past them, is through them.

The beauty of space and silence. It's really home.

A place where nothing more needs to be said.

THE PROCESS

In recent years, my writings have slowly built up to help me understand this quest I've been on. Writing helps me put into perspective certain concepts and questions that I have posed to myself, hoping to get my own answers. Writing has helped me solidify my own conclusions.

Please remember that everything that I write about stems from my own experiences. I don't write to change anyone. I am not capable of that. Nor do I ever want to impose my beliefs on anyone else. I began writing, reading spirituality books, and more to help myself understand things.

If you're like me, despite reading all the books in this world, you'll likely find that the only true way to learn and change is through experience. You have to realize things for yourself, embark on a journey that is personal. It's all part of your growth, part of your own distinct path called your life.

On the other hand, along my path, I did realize something very simple yet very profound that has made sharing more meaningful for me: that we are all the same. We all struggle with the same issues and the same insecurities, and we all seek the same basic things, regardless of our race, creed, wealth, sexual orientation, or gender identity.

The only thing we can ever do is change ourselves. And that is where we should focus our energy first to align better with the love we were born to express.

If what I'm covering seems too deep to understand at times, that is okay. I totally can relate to that. I have read some very complicated books over the years, and at times, they went beyond me. Yet I kept going forward. And that is the key: To be relentless in the quest for your desired understanding is the key to success. Never give up! Fear nothing! This has been my motto over the years.

Because of our individual conditioning, we all have different paths we must experience in order to reach the next level of understanding. We each pass through the stages differently. So, what one person goes through is not necessarily what others will need.

Just know that no matter what is in front of you, no matter how bad things seem, you have within you a great source of untapped power that is beyond comprehension. And for most of us, it lies latent our entire lives. I have experienced this power, and it scared me initially, to be truthful. But it led me to inquire about what it is that lies within me.

By having curiosity and courage, you will solidify your new beliefs and become comfortable with new concepts.

Only through this individual process of self-awareness will you really change from living a life to living from Love.

THE TRUTH

Truth. Such a hard concept to grasp. I had avoided questioning my understanding of it for years, avoided what some say is life's most important concept to question. However, let's dive into it!

What is truth? And what does it really mean to you? We all want it. Right? We hate to be lied to. To be deceived. However, truth can indeed be deceitful. My truth is different from yours. My experiences will always be different from yours.

Maybe one person sees a lump of coal and another person sees a diamond in the making. Not something objective, but something subjective.

As I see it, truth is something that's not outside us but rather, it's inside of us. It moves like clouds, like thoughts. A constantly shifting target. Hard to grasp. So, what does truth mean to me?

Truth is who you really are, the beginning and the end. Your intrinsic nature. And it's wondrous. Truth is our internal world where no clouded thoughts linger and the sky is completely clear.

The truth is who we are. That which is. That which I am.

Pure awareness.

Straight from the heart.

THE POWER OF WORDS

Sometimes when I read certain words, my whole world changes. That's the power of words. One single word can change the course of your entire life. One single sentence can spread your wings to new heights or bring you down to a valley of despair. Words vibrate.

Everything has a vibration, with some things vibrating higher than others. The words of the past that sought higher heights, sought loftier goals, continue to vibrate in the present. Because the best words speak to an ideal we can all aspire to. Because deep inside us, that ideal is already there.

In the Bible, the first verse in the opening chapter of the Gospel according to John begins with this one powerful sentence: "In the beginning was the word, and the word was God." There is no more powerful sentence than that. Because it's so true.

It all begins with a thought. A word.

What you think. What you declare. What you say.

Is what you become.

KNOWING GOD

God is our highest instinct to know ourselves.

—DEEPAK CHOPRA

One day, I was driving down a long stretch of road in the dry, golden hills of eastern Washington when I had an interesting epiphany. After all this investigation and reflecting, I realized that my belief in what you might call God or infinite intelligence is exactly the relationship I have with myself.

The infinite is within and also without; what we think within and about ourselves will be reflected in the world we experience. That is, how we approach the world shapes what experiences we get back from it, shapes our life.

Now, this is completely opposite of what you might think: that God or this higher power is somewhere out there. But as I've mentioned before, we are a mirror. We reflect that which we are. Most of us have heard the saying that man was made in the mirror image of God; thus, we are God. So, if this is correct, the inverse also holds true: that which we are is reflected back to us. I know this may seem tough to grasp because I'm flipping this concept; however, that slight change refocuses your worldview quite profoundly.

Which brings me to one of the most amazing books I have ever read. It wasn't a coincidence that right after that God-within-me epiphany, I revisited the very book that would explain the concept above more clearly. You may read something one day and then reread it later and, because of new experiences, you will understand it better. You will get more out of it.

Over the years, I had read Deepak Chopra a few times before when I came across *How To Know God* in a library. When I read it, I thought, *Wow! How can someone have so much insight into this? How could someone put it into words?*

As I mentioned, in the mystery schools, you pass certain levels on your quest to the top of the pyramid, and each level builds upon the previous one. What Chopra does in this particular book is describe seven different stages of a human being's spiritual evolution.

The timing of reading this was serendipitous because it was the five-year anniversary of this part of my journey, and close to Christmas, which I use as a time of reflection.

To me, the birth of Christ that Christmas honors represents what Jesus' message was all about. As you may know, Jesus is called by many Jesus "The Christ." The ending "Christ" part refers to a Christ Consciousness or

God Consciousness. Jesus, Buddha, and Mohammed all represent this high level of spiritual development.

Chopra writes that each stage of God represents your relationship to reality. Each stage is a world unto itself. Most of us live in Stage One or Stage Two, where experiences of fear, survival, dependency, control, and false power are a focus. Very few make it past these levels. However, it is possible to mature to the next stages, past projection. Actually, this is the road we're all traveling whether we realize this or not.

Each stage is a psychological shift—a shift within the mind. These repeated shifts paradoxically lead us to a state of "no mind." Pure consciousness. Christ consciousness.

It's an amazing world out there, truly awe-inspiring. We are all capable of great things, tremendous things. But in the end, it is up to us to get there. To see the endless possibilities that exist right in front of us, in this moment.

Many believe they have seen it all, that there is nothing new to create or explore. Yet everything you see around you, like a chair or a tree outside, was nothing but a possibility once. A possibility that did indeed come true.

You were once a possibility, something that did not exist. However, that possibility, the one that you call "you," beat all the odds and shifted from being a possibility to a living truth.

Your new world awaits. You just need to find the courage to cross the boundaries you've accepted that box you into a certain stage of life, to face your fears. In the end, it is your belief in a life in which ego is not in control and where Oneness matters more that will lift you up into the mountains of freedom.

In Oneness lies the key.

CADA CABEZA ES UN MUNDO

Magic doesn't exist only in fairytales. It also exists in this world.

You can't have the good without the bad, though, just as you can't live a life without the reality of eventually dying. You can't "have it all" unless you're willing to lose it all, and you cannot hate someone without first loving them.

A shift in consciousness, a slight change in perspective can open you up to a new world. Regardless of the shift, your world is different from my world, and your neighbor's world is different from everyone else's. "*Cada cabeza es un mundo,*" my grandmother used to tell me. "Every mind is a world." Every mind is a universe unto itself. She was absolutely right.

It makes you wonder, doesn't it? Just how far the rabbit hole goes.

It goes all the way. Farther than you can imagine. However, don't take my word for it. It's up to you to discover this on your own. Because it's your world and no one else's. You're the ruler of your own kingdom.

And you can't have a kingdom without magic.

PART III

MEDITATIONS ON RETURNING

CLEANSING WATERS

Way out past our own level of murky understanding
Past the fears
Past the insecurities
Even past death...
I bravely arrived to a feeling of quiet stillness

A place of golden warm peace.

As the cleansing waters washed over me,
I finally slowly opened my eyes
To this realization of exquisite beauty
That feeling of being acutely and utterly
Alive

To this place
This oasis of life
They call love.

Home.

— Roman

THE HOMECOMING

Who we are looking for is who is looking.

—ST FRANCIS OF ASSISI

Most of us would rather not look back at our supposed bad experiences due to the pain that may arise. Only by looking back and processing repressed pain, though, can we find true healing. Only by cycling back to the past can we get past certain hurdles that may keep us from regaining connection to our authentic self, or true self.

So, what should you do when life throws you an unanticipated challenge? Something you didn't see coming? You have every right to be frustrated and angry initially. However, learn to lean into that as well. Learn to go with the flow of life, for working with past and present tribulations bring some of life's greatest gifts of growth.

But first, there are sorrows. You can't see the mountaintop while still climbing, while still working on yourself or staring at the ending of something like a relationship.

It may even take months—sometimes years—before you can look back at the valley you've traveled and say to yourself, "Yes, now I understand why I needed to go through that situation."

The healing to unbury your authentic self is not easy work, either. That said, if you dare to go that route, you'll find the answer on the path that keeps calling you. Healing old wounds leads to the freedom your soul wants.

By facing emotional wounds, you'll make great strides in life. You'll release the pains of old, freeing up space within you to allow the real you to emerge. Releasing those pains will make you actually feel lighter. You'll also feel your center of being grow.

Addressing past wounds actually helps you feel more anchored too. Just as a tree is connected to the earth through its roots, so, too, will you become more anchored, or as some put it, more "grounded." That grounding allows you to develop real confidence.

Healing is all about reconnecting to our true selves. In studying psychology, I learned the concept of the "inner child," the little boy or girl we lost as we grew up. The part of us that lives predominantly in the present moment. You can see it in the awe in the eyes of a child of less than three or four years. Just watch them play.

Over time, though, life has a way of wounding us. Life shackles our little wonder child, the part of us we're really looking for. As we grow up, we experience emotional trauma that can sometimes remain buried as we grow older, manifesting in fear, anxiety, and unhappiness. If we grew up in a household with abusive parents, with alcoholics, or with adults who had anger issues, this can create especially deep emotional wounds that we as adults need to face and work through.

You are not alone in such struggles, as wounding has been happening to humans for thousands of years. Despite the way technology has improved the outer world, our inner world still needs to be worked on. I remember one night, when I was doing some intense internal work, realizing that the emotional pain we all go through is the exact same pain people have had since the beginning of humanity. Everyone struggles to get past societally learned knowledge that may no longer serve them anymore—to unlearn beliefs and heal parts of the wounded self.

The brilliant author of many self-help books, John Bradshaw, guided me in understanding what those wounded parts consist of. Bradshaw identifies the soul as the wonder child and the ego as our wounded child. He states in *Homecoming* that we need both the wonder child and the ego in order to self-actualize and for individuation to occur during adulthood.

According to him, the wonder child is our true, authentic self. It's our connection back to who we were after being born, the part of us that wants acceptance and understanding. To be loved. Our journey is about freeing ourselves to be who we really are, freeing the childlike soul within through healing work. We need to face the emotional baggage some of us have carried into adulthood and release the pent-up shame, fear, rage, and pain buried deep within.

By doing this internal work to reintegrate the injured parts of ourselves, our wounded child, we then slowly start to become whole and mature. Individuation happens by integrating our different aspects and becoming a mature, self-actualized human being.

In Bradshaw's book, he reiterates that by healing our wounded child (ego), we gain access to our authentic self through the integration process, bringing us to a balanced whole.

After you've reconnected with your authentic self (soul), he believes you can then move on to the second step, during which your ego (mind) becomes a loving parent to your soul, or your wonder child. That's when your internal self-talk starts to change. You know that reversal is underway when you start hearing your internal voice state, "Yes, you can do this," instead of "You can't do anything right." That's where internal compassion and self-love starts to come in. Unconditional love.

Accessing your wonder child also allows you to give love to others. Creativity comes from the freed wonder child as well. You never lost it. It just needed to be actualized.

Bradshaw also notes in his book that you gain a broader perspective after re-awakening your soul. As he writes:

"Once you feel the connection with your wonder child, you begin to see your whole life from a larger perspective. Your wonder child no longer has to hide from ego defenses for survival. He can see things from a different level of consciousness. The wonder child is not a better self; he is a different self with a much larger vision."

I believe this broader connection that comes from overcoming painful memories and liberating your wonder child is when the "I" becomes the "we." When the soul understands itself, it understands that it is indeed part of the whole. A part of the highest level of realization.

Out of chaos, we were created, and out of chaos, we are born anew. We come home again.

THE SEEKER AWAKENS

They say our society is progressing. In one year, our technology now leaps as far as it used to in a hundred years. Technology may be moving fast. Yet what progress are *we* really making? What goal is technology getting us closer to?

Somehow, along the way, we all lost something. And we spend the majority of our lives searching for it. I believe, on the grand scale, what we are all seeking is greater connection.

The more I traveled down this self-development path, the more I realized that we're indeed connected on a deeper level to the forces of what some people refer to as the cosmos. Everything is connected to everything, and the things that I do affect you as the things you do affect me. Though physically we may be removed by miles, at the source, you and I are the same. And will always be. Even beyond what you would call physical death.

What a different world this would be if we all felt this way, if we all realized this. A new, deeper meaning of the word "responsibility" would emerge, and maybe— just maybe—we'd get to that next stage of our personal journeys. It is much easier to blame others, though, when we suffer. You blame others and yourself, thus creating feelings of guilt. However, something profound happens when you stop blaming.

Through the power of forgiveness and self-understanding, you start taking responsibility. Then you start maturing, and things start changing. Little by little, you gain your own power back. You relight your flame. The world gets better. You start to free yourself to be yourself. Without responsibility, there is no freedom.

Essentially, we are all chasing the same thing that is at the heart of connection to the cosmos. It comes down to self-acceptance: Are we willing to accept who we are right now without judging ourselves?

We have been led to believe that we all lack something. We worry that maybe we aren't attractive enough, maybe we don't have what everybody else seems to have. We search for love, for money, for status, for security. We sometimes achieve it, and yet the hole is still there. It seems to never end. When is it enough?

As E.E. Cummings once wrote, "To be nobody-but-yourself—in a world which is doing its best, night and day, to make you everybody else—means to fight the hardest battle which any human being can fight; and never stop fighting."

More so than with anything else I've read, I always return to my favorite story, "The Allegory of the Cave," from

The Republic by Plato. If you can understand that one story, a lot of what I write should make sense. However, to get the most out of Oneness-related concepts, we have to experience them for ourselves. Words mean nothing without the background of individual experience to paint them on.

It's a complicated subject, discussing the true self, because there is no way to really describe it. You have to experience it.

It's like the old analogy: "How does a fish know that it is living in water? Not until the day he jumps out of the water." There's no other way. Secondhand knowledge won't get you there. The true self is something that has to be cultivated in order to attain it.

When you do this type of internal work, you aren't really learning anything you don't already know. The secret is removing the blocks that are holding you back from finding your true self. Your true self already lies within you. That's why the terms "self-development" and "self-help" are inaccurate. The real definition we should be using is "the art of self-remembering." It's a return home to innocence, or what some would call returning to our kingdom.

Your true self is there already inside you. You just have to do the internal work to uncover it.

Is it easy? No, it may be the hardest thing you ever experience. You will have to die a million little deaths; yet every death brings with it new life. Until finally, one day, when you least expect it, the true self shines through, and you align with the freedom that living a soul-focused life brings.

My biggest personal tragedy was my near-death experience. But during that experience, I first realized that I wasn't just my body. I entered a still, timeless space of acute awareness. Yes, it scared me; however, it was also my greatest gift. Because that experience allowed me to quicken my internal journey, to travel up the ladder, to reach personal points I never thought were possible.

And I now know my destiny, for it lies within these words, the gift of giving the words that I give to you. That is why I'm here.

There is a purpose we are all here to fulfill. To reach the level of the soul, the true self, where fear doesn't tread, and every possibility exists. Our shared destiny is the light. Freedom. Joy.

Ultimately, it's better known as the word "Love." To enter into that beautiful responsibility. What we seek, we already have. We already are. It can just take a bit of a struggle to figure it out. But the struggle is well worth it. And when you arrive, you will laugh at the whole comedic tragedy. Ha! Just as Buddha did when he became enlightened underneath the Bodhi Tree.

I believe that you will find your true self in the last place you would think to look. Not outside yourself, but within.

We only arrive when there is nothing left for us to seek.

ETERNITY AND
THE DIMENSIONS OF TIME

I used to ponder the word "eternity." I always wondered what it meant. We've heard that real love lasts forever, that real love is eternal. But what does that mean?

And should we associate eternity, infinity, with heaven? After contemplating this further, I came to the realization that eternity is not permanence. Eternity is depth. It isn't permanence that I'm after. It's really depth. And how many people live a life of depth?

Have you ever seen something or experienced something so beautiful it left you breathless? Have you ever looked into the eyes of another, into the great mysterious depth that lies in their eyes? The awe-inspiring, deep resonance of something beautiful you can somehow feel but cannot quite grasp?

It's there, I tell you. It's there. It's life's depth you experience in those speechless moments where time does not seem to exist. A taste of divine love.

That beautiful dive into the eternal. That mesmerizing silence.

It's taken me over a decade to come to terms with "eternity" as a word that encompasses everything, yet nothing. For eternity is really a return to nothingness. A limitless place of pure consciousness.

I once heard an old story about the cross, one with a different meaning than what most of us associate with Christianity. The cross symbolized time. And time to most of us moves horizontally, forward from yesterday to today to tomorrow. That's the horizontal bar.

So, what does the vertical bar mean then? What of time and its depth?

Life doesn't truly move sideways or horizontally. It stacks one moment on top of the other. A vertical motion. We're moving down, or we're moving up. Our ancestors may have understood this reality better. They understood that time also has depth. Likewise, the vertical bar on the cross runs deep.

It's also not time that's moving; it is us. The ever-present moment always stands still. And it always will. It's what they call the moment. Beyond yesterday. Beyond tomorrow. The eternal moment. You see, there is no yesterday; there is no tomorrow. It's all a big façade. Yesterday is just a memory, and tomorrow is a dream.

Time never moves to a "there." It is we who are moving. It is the planets that are moving.

And we can choose: to live in the horizontal, or better yet, to live vertical. Because the moment has depth.

Don't let the practice of stepping into the moment become something you get around to doing someday.

Because someday never will come.

When we fully accept our experience in the present moment, there is no time. It's just pure awareness. It's freedom. It's light. It's the only place you can experience divine love.

Heaven is right here, right now. It's something the mind will never really grasp. Because it goes beyond the mind. But it can be experienced.

Why wait? Why wait to go home? Why not live there now?

Eternity on the edge of your every breath.

LIFTING THE VEIL OF ILLUSION

Sometimes I look around and see so much unhappiness, loneliness, and depression that I wonder, *Who is happy?* I see people who smile on the outside, yet the smile isn't real. I've done that myself. It's tragic, isn't it, to live life like this? A lie at its most extreme. But that is how this world usually works.

We are taught that in order to be happy, we must accomplish this or that. We are taught to not show how we really feel because it may offend someone. These ideas are so ingrained in us that we don't question the insanity of living like this. Our life can seem like a never-ending battle of trying to keep up an illusion.

The most fearful thing is to be found out, for people to see beyond our masks.

I've noticed over the years that many of us tend to hold back our truth. We at times fail to speak our truth, and truth to me means more than words. It's also action. We all want to be liked. Really, we all want to be loved.

Love is out there, we think, and what do we need to do

to get it? We tend to believe we need to conform to what other people think in order to be loved. Even if it means holding back our own truth.

Thus, fear of becoming separated from the love outside of us stands in the way of our love.

Yet no one can ever give us that feeling of being loved. It's a feeling that we ourselves create, something internal. The fire.

Yes, someone can fan it. Yes, someone can make it grow for a little bit, but sooner or later, it recedes to our own internal thermometer. Our own internal limit. And who sets your limit? Who controls it?

It's you.

There is a point along the self-development path for those who have decided they no longer want to suffer. They decide to take matters into their own hands. The rebels! And they go out and seek their own knowledge, their own truth.

Some of us seek to improve our lives by making changes, reading books, or adapting new theologies. However, the core of what everyone is searching for is what we are already. It isn't self-improvement that we must do. Instead, it's chipping away everything you have ever learned. We all seek to build upon what we have learned, yet it escapes us that we should be chipping away at our perceptions of reality instead.

What you seek, you already are. Enlightenment isn't just for Buddha or Jesus or Mohammed. And that is what these masters tried to teach us. This is the core of their teachings. Enlightenment is your birthright; it is your ultimate destiny. Your ultimate flowering.

We all have a fire. A light. Our truth. Love.

You can choose to let this flame flicker all your life— to wither and bend at the mercy of the wind—or you can choose to stand up and feed that flame, to see how high you can get it burning. So, don't hold back. Damn the fear!

Let your flame shine through. Live to burn higher. Live to burn brighter.

In turn, someday your flame will burn so bright that you will be able to help others.

The veil of illusion can be pierced. The veil will fall away as truth is revealed. The key is to believe that it is possible. For in possibility lies opportunity. And if that is what you seek, someday you will indeed arrive, whether in this lifetime or in your next.

But why wait to experience your true, authentic self? To dance the dance only you came here to do? Why wait to be free? Liberation is yours! Take it!

Be the light you came here to be.

LEARNING TO LOVE YOURSELF

It is indeed true that we're all on different paths. Some of us are growing in leaps and bounds; others struggle to move forward. Yet a cup of water from the sea is still part of the sea, part of the whole, still the same essence. So, one path is not better than any other. All rivers eventually lead back to the sea.

Ultimately, I do believe that our path is about learning to love ourselves. To be love itself. I once did an exercise where I wrote down all the qualities I liked in another person. After it was done, I looked down at my list and thought, *Wow, this sounds a lot like me!* And I laughed. Because the list was a reflection of who I thought I was. This crazy exercise had tremendous value, for it reminded me that we tend to see life as we see ourselves. Our perceptions color our worlds as they color the perceptions of others we encounter.

Along this road of life, you're going to meet a lot of resistance, even from those you hold most dear. However, this path is your own. It's about you.

Our personal experiences continuously shape each of us. What works for one may not work for another. We all do the best we can, given what we have. If we all truly understood that, this world would indeed be heaven.

At the same time, we are all indeed One. We can learn from each other, and that to me is the beauty of our different paths. We all have something to give, something to share.

I believe deep down most of us feel a longing, and we might not know why. Sometimes some of us even feel a hole within us. Usually, after we have lost something or someone, this hole becomes more apparent. You are not alone, though. There are many of us in the same situation. We have this internal yearning to return to something we think we might have lost. But how can we miss something if we've never had it before? How can that be?

Because maybe we just can't see it yet. Or maybe we have forgotten. It's up to us to remember, and we can. And ultimately, we will.

Stick to your path. Follow your inspiration, whatever it is that gives you life. Follow your inner light, for it always leads home.

This is your journey. Your ride. Start rowing!

Start rowing home.

TO REFLECT LIKE A MIRROR

The analogy of the mirror occurs and resonates across cultures. We find this analogy in many different philosophies, especially Zen. But what does it really mean to live like a mirror?

A mirror reflects exactly what is in front of it. It makes no judgment. It lives in the moment and responds to whatever we place in front of it. If you place your hand in front of it, the mirror will reflect your hand. If you put a flower in front of it, it will reflect a flower. It does not reflect something in the past or future. It focuses on what is in front of it. Totally fresh, totally new, each time.

We can see this same ability to focus in the present with one- or two-year-old children. They respond totally to the moment like a mirror. Age has nothing to do with it, though. It is the mind that makes the choice.

Living in the moment can make every moment totally young, totally new, and totally present. We can then see the world again through eyes of wonder. And we merge with existence because existence only happens now. It has no past and no future. It just is. Just like a reflection in a mirror.

THE ACT OF CREATING

It's interesting how you can read something over and over and still not really get it until maybe the umpteenth time. Repetition has a purpose. In part, our perspective changes with time so that deeper meaning can emerge. Your view of the world now is not the same as it was ten years ago, last year, or even last week. We're all changing in some way or another. However, it seems to me that in order to accelerate our expansion, we must consciously choose to repeat activities as if doing them for the first time, making each a new experience.

Our greatest teachings come in everyday interactions, in life. You can read something, yet when you face it in the field of life, the experience burns into you, molding who you are and how you view things.

If you spend enough time studying yourself and the world, you come to realize that there are Laws of Nature. We use these laws every day, but many are not really aware of all of them.

You may have heard of alchemy as some far-off fantasy, a myth of medieval times in which people would seek to transform other metals into gold. Yet spiritual alchemists using the true Laws of Nature are what we are. We live in a world of magic and are capable of things beyond the scope of our sometimes-limited imagination. In particular, we are constantly creating, moment by moment, our experiences in this life.

So, you hold the power to create what you want to experience. To be free to enjoy this world and experience this wonderful feeling of being alive. The power has always been yours. The power has always been within.

The power, of course, is love.

Which brings me back to staying aware of each moment, the place where we can consciously choose to create what we really want. Where the act of creating lies.

Many have read about the Law of Attraction (that which is like unto itself, is drawn). Yet you may not get how it really works. My personal belief is that right now, we are indeed creating our own life experience whether we're conscious of it or not. So, if this is true...why not choose to do it consciously?

Why not choose to have an experience you want as opposed to one you don't? That's essentially what a lot of the books I've read over the years are really saying. Though I was skeptical of this initially, over time, I have become more comfortable with that and other ideas. Of course, I take what works and forget the rest. And later, if it stops working, I change it again.

We live in a world full of contrasts. For example, sometimes we have to experience what we don't want in order to appreciate, and create a desire for, what we do want.

We are continually growing at the forefront, the leading edge of life's expansion. You could say that the universe is expanding through us. We are creating just like the universe and in nature/life. So, if this is the case, everything that exists or will exist is already within our grasp. It's just a matter of tuning in to it, thereby attracting it into your experience.

Yet how do you know you are creating what's wanted? By how you feel. If it feels good, you're on the right track. If not, you need to get back on track. Pay attention to how you feel.

By sending an intention of what you want, you are asking the universe for something. Then you must let the universe do the work on its own. We must trust that our intention will happen and not worry about the details.

We must allow ourselves to experience what we want to create. This is a tough one to grasp because most of us say we want something, yet deep down, we don't think we deserve to be connected to it. That's resistance. And where does most of our resistance come from? Others in our path who have told us, "No, you can't do that," or "No, that's wrong." We've been trained to hold back. Actually, we've been trained to give our power away. Crazy, isn't it?

We came here with a lot of power. We came here as

creators, but along the path, we lost our power. Or we think we've lost it. The truth is, you still have it. You just need to realize it for yourself.

Essentially that is what my writings are all about. To help you get back to who you really are. And who you really are is much greater, much more powerful than what you may think.

Everything in this world is a vibration. You are a vibration. This is a scientific fact. According to quantum physics, you are vibrating in and out of existence as you read this. Within that infinite soup of vibration lies the creation you want to give birth to, something you would love to experience. What you need to do is believe that you can make it come to fruition. Match your internal vibration to the vibration you seek to experience, and sooner or later it will be drawn into your life.

Gratitude is the final piece to the puzzle. Gratitude keeps you in the flow of what comes next. It is like feeling grateful for the river of your life that you have already experienced and expecting to have more to be grateful for down the path you have yet to see.

Don't get caught up in the snags your life experience has brought. Have faith that the river of life will keep you moving to the goal you really desire. Remember, you get what you focus on. If you focus on and complain about an experience, the focus on that negative "reality" will most likely cause that vibration, that reality, to persist. Choose what you want and stick to that intention. Focus on what you want, not on what you don't want. Sooner or later, it will come to fruition.

It's not the physical object or result you're really after. It's the internal feeling you get from them.

This is law.

The Law of Attraction.

The conscious act of creating.

PERSONAL FREEDOM

Many times in my life I have heard people say, "This is what I want for you," or "This is what is best for you," or "This is what you should do." And deep inside, these pronouncements have always made me angry. We hear these statements from our parents, grandparents, teachers, partners, and bosses.

Who are they to tell you what to do? Who are they to create your dream? They may mean well, but their intentions have nothing to do with you.

You have within you an internal guidance system quite capable of making decisions. The system is called your emotions. Your emotions will let you know what is true for you, what is right for you.

Would a king or queen give their power away? Never let anyone do so to you. Neither I nor anyone else. There are no outside experts in this world, for this world is your world. Your kingdom.

True freedom does not exist out there in physical space. A man locked in a cell can have more real freedom than most people in this world. For true freedom lies within. This is what you're chasing. The courage to finally be yourself, which is the key to lasting happiness.

Only you know what your essential hopes, your dreams are. Understanding them is your truth. Your freedom. Your life!

You can never go wrong expressing who you truly are.

EMOTIONS AS OUR GUIDE

In today's society, most of us tend to use reason and logic—in other words, our minds—as the gauge that forms the foundation for our reality. Operating from an individualized, logical mind is just how our society has evolved.

Yet if you really want to live, to taste this thing I call life, you have to bring emotion into it. You have to go by what you feel, even though you've been taught otherwise. We've been told to stuff our emotions inside. To not show them. To be stoic. To keep it together. Damn, how sad is that?

Emotions are an important part of life. They provide the myriad colors of this reality you're living right now. Emotions are what give you the feeling of being alive. Most of us run from our feelings, not so much the good ones but the bad ones. We hold them inside. And that is the worst thing to do.

I know I have done that most of my life. I have stuffed them inside me. And it's funny where they've resided. They're usually in my stomach area. Yet they can be anywhere in the body. They can manifest as disease. Dis-Ease. Uneasiness. And it's toxic. It sometimes even kills people.

"Emotion." Let's break this word down. It's E (Energy)-in-motion. Energy. An emotion has to be felt in order to be acknowledged. Yet we've learned to ignore them, to stuff them inside, to not acknowledge them. I've been there. I've been down that path. I have felt the weight of years of holding an emotion in until it manifested as deep anxiety and even panic attacks. I have carried emotional baggage for many years within me. We all have, to some degree or another. And sometimes it takes years to let emotions go.

However, sometimes, when the pressure gets too much, the valve breaks, and we explode. Through anger, through grief, through tears of long-forgotten pain.

You can't hide from feelings. They and their energy are still there. Energy never dies. It just transforms.

You do have a wonderful option to transform them on your terms, I tell you. To let it all go. To acknowledge a grief, a burdening energy, and then to let it leave your body. To say, "Yes!" to it. To bring it to the light and let it fly into the wind.

Because that's all the grief or other emotion really wanted in the first place. It just wanted to be acknowledged. It wanted to be felt.

That, to me, is regaining our power.

I know this power from my own reckonings with it.

After my near-death accident and all the physical

injuries I had gone through, I held both the physical and emotional pains inside me for five rough years. At the time, I believed a true person of strength would just keep going, pain and all. I had refused to see a doctor after the accident and instead, hobbled around for months while the entire left side of my body had major soft tissue injuries and the hematomas in my leg finally dissipated.

On top of that, working in a highly stressful new sales job assaulted my body with stress hormones. It all finally culminated in panic attacks and ongoing physical ailments, until finally, the physical pain led me to the right doctor. He finally showed me in a mirror just how bad my soft tissue injuries were. There was a big difference between the size of my left shoulder and my right shoulder—my left was very, very inflamed. I took a lot of pain medication and did deep tissue work, which slowly, over time, helped. Yet that emotional pain was still inside of me.

Finally, there came a night when I'd had enough of the suffering. The tipping point was when a relationship came to a heartrending end. I lost the person closest to me in my life up to that point, and it hit me deep and hard.

But the light inside of that pain was that I had finally had enough. I released a lot of other things I had been carrying inside me. In early December of 2002, my life after the near-death experience reached a tumultuous point. These strange feelings boiled out of me. I felt searing fear and anxiety. It erupted like a volcano from deep within my being. And at first, I had no idea I had been carrying this within me. My body, convulsing with deep emotions, and my awareness, just watching the emotions pour out of me. It was one of the most horrid—yet uplifting—experiences I have ever had to go through. The valve holding back those emotions could no longer withstand any more pressure and had finally opened.

I could feel the emotional pain leave my body, the weight of its release. Out of something really bad, something even better was birthed. To this day, I see that point in my life as a gift. For if I hadn't gone through it, I would still be carrying the pain today. And these writings would have never been created.

If you can learn to acknowledge and release your emotions, you will learn to live in a different realm. You will merge fully with each present moment.

To feel alive...to acknowledge the feeling in your heart and the life that its pumping sustains. It is here in this moment. In this present moment of feeling. The feeling of magic...the feeling of who we are...the true beauty of love. Love for ourselves and love for anything that was and ever will be.

Energy is life: the energy you came from, the energy you are, and the energy you will one day return to. Dance with it! Let the colors of emotions move through you...let them color your world. And like the true artist that you are, use these paints to create this masterpiece called your life.

ALIVENESS

Sometimes we feel more alive and sometimes less so, regardless of age or how healthy we are. It isn't the body that really gauges our quality of life. It's our state of consciousness. Our current state of vibration.

The people we love to hang out with are the ones with higher vibrational energy, that stunning energy we want to be a part of. Something we don't want to be without it. A gorgeous magnet calling us ever closer to that feeling we are searching for. They draw out our aliveness from deep within us. That feeling of happiness we yearn for.

They become a fire that feeds the flicker of our flame. We are aching to taste that feeling of aliveness, of blissful happiness.

My near-death experience left me with a taste of something that will never leave me. And so, afterward, I went searching for that moment's meaning. It was an ineffable experience that I struggled to describe in words.

An ocean adventurer helped me find my way. I have been fascinated by waves ever since I was a kid. The rhythm, the aliveness, the soothing sound of water in movement. Then one day, I listened to an interview by a famous surfer, and I understood what I was struggling to grasp about how it felt to have that watery brush with death.

The surfer's specialty was riding big waves. At one point, he had held the record for surfing a hundred-foot wave. Imagine seeing this huge wave coming down on top of you—and being at the edge of it. It sounds crazy. For someone to go and search for it and put themselves in that type of danger seems extreme. He said he wanted to feel that aliveness that danger brings. That moment where everything else shrinks, and it's just you and that edge. And damn, isn't that just awesome? Isn't that just bold! I was like, *Yes!* This is that moment of creativity. Where someone gets lost in their art and merges into what is.

I realized after much searching, that that beautiful space I touched while close to death was nothing more than being in the presence of who I truly am, of stepping into the core of my being. The experience of totally feeling alive.

Yet we do not have to go to extremes, such as I did, to find deeper meaning. Aliveness is an art we can learn to cultivate, that blissful feeling we experience when we totally get enraptured in the moment. Whatever makes us come alive is an endeavor worth pursuing.

What's crucial is whether you step out and surf that wave that only you were meant to ride. That you put yourself into that moment when you internally smile and say, "Yes! Yes! I'm doing this!"

In such moments of exuberance, of total expansion, a feeling will come over you. A swelling from within. You will have stepped onto the creative edge where we all can actually live. This feeling where there is no death. This moment of aliveness. This full state of bliss.

Dive deeper into your aliveness now, and you will vibrate at a higher level.

Feel that internal sun that you have within.

THE SOUL'S DREAM

A long time ago, I met a soul whose life was nothing but play: a radiant dream, a masterpiece of art. This soul had aspirations; nothing held it back. Nothing but freedom did this soul experience. A beautiful dance.

You could see it in its eyes, the fire of a million suns. The soul's fire showed through, illuminating the world from the inside out. This soul knew freedom! This soul new life! Most importantly, this soul knew unconditional love.

For it understood that life came from one source. And that was love itself. It trusted life. It said, "Yes!"

Sadly, the soul came to believe the outside world more than it did its own internal knowing. And it got lost for a moment. A momentary loss occurred in the grand song it came here to sing. Yet it was only momentary.

For the soul came to understand in its due time that it was never lost in the first place. It was only lost in another dream. A dream not of its own making. Someone else's dream, someone else's story. That momentary loss was the experience the soul needed to find its way back to its true self, its true home. For the soul could never come to understand itself unless it understood what it was not.

That is our story. The story of you and me. For that dream, that aspiration, that seed of creation still lies dormant within you. You indeed are the artist of your life! A master painter. Your birthright! Your dream.

A beautiful soul waiting to sing your authentic song.

—

PART IV

MEDITATIONS OF REVEALING

THE BEAUTY BEYOND THE MIND

One day we are going to look back
at our own personal movie
To see what played on our screen

The highs, the lows
The tragedies and the triumphs,
The pain and the ecstasy

The deep well of inexhaustible creativity.

The adventure of life makes for great drama
A great story.

But who we really are is beyond that

Beyond the sea of emotions
Beyond the mind
Beyond the body
Lies a great mystery
An immovable seer watching it all pass by

And that's the beauty of you and I.

Something to awaken to
One day,
One day.
Let that day

Be today.

— Roman

AN INSPIRING NEW WORLD

"Inspired." Let's break down that word for a minute. "In spirit." That's where the word comes from. To live in accordance with your spirit.

We tend to believe that we are separate from everyone else. On the outside, yes, we all look different. We come in many different shapes, colors, and sizes. But at our core, are we really? Inside, we are all made of the same essence. The same divine nature. At the center, we all have a soul, and our soul is an individuation of the whole. God's essence.

In the flowering of our possibility, we start to navigate new unchartered personal waters in which we increase our capacity to love. We start realizing deeper expressions of our essence. Releasing more and more of our individual fragrance of this thing called love, which allows us to create a new world.

It's a world of unlimited possibilities, of uttermost freedom. It's where I'm allowed to be me, and you're allowed to be you—regardless of how we look or what status we hold in the outside world.

What an interesting place earth would be if that were to happen. A place where all the lines blur and we all become One in spirit. You would be tempted to call it heaven.

Connecting to Oneness is a shift, just a little shift in approach that can happen at any moment. Take a look around you, at the beauty around you in people's eyes. What do you see? Maybe, just maybe...you see yourself?

Life recognizing life itself. To finally awaken to the truth. To live in spirit with all.

Now that would be inspiring.

WE ARE ARTISTS

It seems that some of the most creative and gifted of us often have the most suffering. Some of these passionate, tortured souls chose to leave us early.

It's tragic, because these artists, poets, writers, musicians, and others left us with only a little bit of their magic, sometimes just enough to tease us, to leave us wondering what more they could have given. What more did they have to say? I wonder what more Jimi Hendrix, Amy Winehouse, and Kurt Cobain could have shared with the world.

Yet we are blessed that they had something profound to say in the first place. Even if they only gave us one song, one book, one poem, that may be all someone else needed to experience to change the direction of their life. One word spoken at the most opportune time can change worlds.

We all have this gift. We are all artists, mystics, alchemists. We all hold magic inside us. We have that power, the power of an artist. The power of a magician.

I have met people in my life—some only once maybe, or very briefly—on road trips, on airplanes, and on the street. People whose names I never internalized. But some of these people left a mark on me. Some, even though they never said a word. I'm sure you've had that experience as well.

Maybe you're not famous. Maybe you don't realize that you have written something memorable—yet.

We are all artists, though. We are all creators in a sense that you may not have considered.

There are really two types of artists in this world: You are an artist of love, or you are an artist of fear. They represent two sides of the same coin. The beauty of being a world-creating artist is...we get to choose.

LET THE WATER RISE

Sometimes we feel the waters of life rise just a little higher than our comfort zone. At times it can feel beyond our capacity to handle, as if we won't be able to float or to keep swimming upward. We want to give up.

However, it's at this point that, if you can hang on just a little longer, you will grow. You will acclimate to the new level you seek. Water always brings us up to its own level.

The secret: Nothing is given to you that deep down you didn't ask for. In other words, this moment, no matter how challenging, is exactly what you need. Some might say I'm crazy. They'll give me worst-case scenarios that no one could possibly choose to manifest.

Yet diving into the moment without judging it, however bad it may seem from your current perspective, will alleviate this dilemma. Accepting the moment as it is is our path to freedom.

The water rises in stages, like water in a canal that's eased upward by the canal locks. It will raise you to one level for a while. Yet there is always another level to climb. It never truly ends.

But damn, the ride does get stranger as you rise to a higher level of water, each more exquisite than the last. The feeling of unity comes into play more and more, the feeling that the water is nothing more than me coming home to myself. It's electrifying to feel. There is no loneliness here.

Let the water carry you up. Go with the flow of what your soul wants! For there is no death, only transformation. And that transformation is all up to you. Do you want freedom? Or do you want what you have now?

So, I say to you, if it must, let the water rise. Let the water take you to the next level. Don't fight it. Don't cling to the past.

Let the movement of the water take you to worlds you have yet to see. To the light that gets you closer to home. To the world of unity, of love. Of everything that was and everything that will ever be.

LIFE KEEPS MOVING

I have heard many people ask, "Remember when?" and recall days of their lost youth. We all do it. We hear that college and high school are the best times of our lives and buy into the idea that it's all downhill from there. The possibilities for growth, for expansion, are out there, though, long after high school ends.

Aging does not have to be about coming to an end, despite the big deal made of aging in our society: The elderly can sometimes be discarded while youthfulness is lifted up onto a pedestal. It's youth we think we must have, and beauty. Both are supposedly synonymous. We believe we have limited time to take advantage of our youth. We must do everything now—or else.

Chronological age really doesn't matter. I have seen people at age ninety bring so much energy to a room as to lift it into the air, and I have seen twenty-year-olds and teenagers so burdened that the room sinks.

It helps to recall the famous words of Marcus Aurelius: that a baby who dies and a ninety-five-year-old who dies actually lose the same thing: the moment. The eternal moment.

The now.

And what about the beauty that comes from experience? The beauty of aging gracefully? I once visited my ninety-three-year-old grandmother who at the time still lived on our family farm in the Yakima Valley. It was a Saturday morning, and I got up expecting to see her in the kitchen. Since she wasn't there in my aunt's house where she was then living, I ventured outside to look for her throughout the numerous old barns and garages. I finally found her about seventy-five yards away in a patch of land where her old farmhouse had once stood.

This was where she had resided for fifty-plus years, raised her children, her grandchildren, and even her great-grandchildren. She'd found out she'd lost a young son there during the Vietnam War era. She had lost her husband on this same farm in a tragic death in the back corral some twenty years prior.

Her two-story yellow house had burned down two years earlier. Nothing was left by the fire. No possessions. No family photos. Gone were her sons' army uniforms and many family heirlooms. The only thing she managed to save was her great grandchild who happened to be there that morning. While the fire raged throughout the house, she got the child out. And that, of course, was enough.

When I found her that morning in her lovely dress

with a blue flower pattern, she stood near where her home once stood, doing something she had done for decade upon decade. Some of the burnt rubble was still visible around her feet.

It was only mid-morning, but the temperature was already almost eighty degrees. And there she was, tending to her rose plants with a hoe in a shaded area, underneath a partially burnt tree.

I was in awe. I just stood and humbly watched. This to her was still her beauty, her life. And nothing was going to stop her from continuing to move forward, to find beauty amidst the destruction. For she totally understood that life keeps on rolling. The roses will one day bloom again.

DEFINING SUCCESS

"Success." Wow, what a crazy, powerful word. It's something that's been defined for us since we were very young. Society wants us to believe success is the huge house, the fancy car, the perfect, trim body, and the high-status job. And because of this, we tend to continuously compare ourselves with others.

But can those hallmarks of "success" withstand the test of time? It's a no-win situation. So, again, what is success? Do you succeed by overworking yourself to have a full bank account? Or do you succeed by raising a child to live free on his or her own? What means more to you? What means more to society?

How can you buy real, lasting success and happiness?

The truth is, you can't. It's impossible. Success and happiness can be fleeting. For tomorrow brings yet another desire. We never quite seem to arrive. Success seems to be right around a continuous corner.

What a bummer. I've been there—having everything society said I should have. Was it liberating? Not really. I actually felt worse than before because I had reached that point that I was told was where I needed to be. Yet I felt empty. I also worried about losing what I had acquired.

I think we have to search for our own success. We have to define our own success. That should really mean more to us. My term for success will be slightly different from yours.

Ralph Waldo Trine wrote, "Do you want to be a power in the world? Then be yourself."

I suspect all healthy definitions of success revolve around feeling more real, more authentic. "Authenticity" is a more fulfilling measure in my mind of success. It means being true to our own selves regardless of what things we may have. Regardless of what people say. It means just plain being happy and comfortable in our own skin.

When someone has that real-ness, we can all sense it. We know what's real. Even if we chose to keep our masks on, some people would be able to see behind the façade, which is our biggest fear.

Worst of all, we know it's a façade.

So, instead, be true. True to yourself. And maybe you will help the world finally reach a better definition of success.

THE ART OF ACTIVE LISTENING

It's an interesting world we live in, where conversational snippets are the norm. Where active listening has become an art you have to practice.

They say we now receive five times as much information every day as we did on a typical day in 1986. And I, too, deal with this overload daily, hourly, by the minute. There's never a dull moment.

Yet those surface moments fly by. But to what end? With what do we feed our minds, our souls? In what ways do we expand?

There's beauty in slowing down, a sort of grace in taking it all in. Of listening to someone completely, without any thought. Of really being there in that moment. It's tough. I know it's tough. However, it's a form of meditation. Mindfulness.

Being in a meditative state allows you to lose yourself in something other than you. You merge with it. You feel it.

Empathy lives here. It's powerful. It's magical. It's a practice. But it's a craft worth its time.

When you truly connect and listen in this way, time ceases to exist. Time does not exist in an intoxicating conversation, in two minds melding as One. Time does not exist in a moment of following your true passion or of just being with someone you love. Connection with the moment becomes a form of mindful meditation.

Patience is power. Silence is golden. Stillness has its place. Connection lies in the here and now. In the moment where time ceases to exist.

CHANGING OUR WORLD

There comes a point along this path we call life where we can sit down and be spectators and watch all that is wrong with this world. Or we can collectively make a change.

We're at this point now. It's a decision that we can hold ourselves accountable for. For we have a unique opportunity today, in this very moment, to stop complaining. To quit being victims and instead understand that this world is really a reflection of us. We truly live in a world that mirrors what we project into it. The reflection of everything we see is like water reflecting ourselves back to us.

Sometimes things happen that totally sideswipe you or come at you in an unexpected way, making you realize how little control you have or how little your understanding of others is. And it's shocking. It makes us feel that we may have no control at all. Or that what we thought to be true may not be true at all. It gives us a helpless feeling. We wonder: Why me? We wonder: How come?

I think these moments are great opportunities to slow

the whole thing down. To realize bigger things, to realize that what we call our normal life is much more than normal. It's an opportunity...a gift.

We are the directors of this movie we call our life, and at some point, we realize we did have something to do with what happened to us. And that moment will be our day of liberation. The day we finally take full responsibility for whatever it is that has transpired.

Most people give their power away and look outside themselves for validation. However, what we look for elsewhere lies deep within us. And when we realize this, we will finally become free.

It was Jesus who once said, "Ye are all gods. And all of you sons of the Most High." He was right. Because you hold within you a divine freedom, your birthright. Your destiny! So, never cower before what you face; never be meek in front of anything that comes in front of you, because you are much more than you realize.

You have what you've been searching for: the power to create that which you came here to create. Most of all, the power to bring happiness to others. And that power I'm talking about can only come now. Because only in the now can you truly create your new tomorrow. It all starts right here, right now, this minute, this second.

Grasp it! Own it! Own it all.

When you do, this world will indeed change. For in order to be the light you came here to become, you must have something or someone to reflect it on. In turn, the light will reflect back to you. The mirror effect.

Let that light be you.

THE FLOW

It's taken me ten years to feel comfortable with automatic writing, the kind where you're not thinking, you're just flowing. Your fingers have a heck of a time keeping up with the flow of the words. When that happens, you know it's going to be good. It just pours out of you.

So, in a sense, it's not really me who drafted these meditations and poems you're reading. It was something greater than myself. Something higher working through me. I also know that for me, the automatic writing comes when it wants. I really don't have a choice but to write. And if I miss the opportunity to put it down on paper, it's gone forever. There are many poems I've written in my head while driving. I wish I would have captured those words. So, I truly honor the opportunity to write whenever it comes—2:00 a.m., 4:00 a.m., whenever. I just do it now.

I suspect everyone has experienced the flow at least once, or what some refer to as "the zone," that experience when they're not thinking, just doing. Creativity becomes more free-flowing. Maybe a great business idea came to you early in the morning, or maybe you lose yourself painting at 3:00 a.m. while the rest of the world is asleep.

Athletes have mentioned being in the zone during their peak performances, and scientists go through this experience before major breakthroughs.

Scientists' latest term to describe this state is "transient hypofrontality." This involves slowing down our prefrontal cortex, the part of our brain where higher cognitive functions happen. This area of our brain is what we use for self-monitoring and where our "inner critic" resides. During a flow state, we deactivate this critic part of our brain to create a more free-flowing state, allowing us to process information faster and focus better. We plunge deeper into the moment.

While problem-solving, you try to contemplate things in your head analytically. Oscillating between thinking and not thinking, between thought and silence. Then at some point, you just let go of the "trying" part. Later, at some peaceful moment, out of the silence, a solution comes to you—like a flash of lightning.

You'd be surprised what else happens when you flow with life. The world will speak to you too. You may hear the answer from where you least expect it. You just have to create the environment to allow it to happen

I didn't choose to become an author. I never had the intention of doing that. It chose me. So, I'm rolling with it. And has it ever been interesting and extremely rewarding—worth every frustrating moment I have encountered while following this calling.

I believe you, too, will find the same feelings if you follow that which calls to your joy.

Life is calling. It calls on you every day, every minute. Calls on you to step into that golden moment when you're allowing life to work through you. We're all life expressing itself in a peak experience of this moment we call now. The question comes down to whether or not we are consciously present to each moment.

Meditation, contemplation, mindfulness, alone time with nature, moments of quietness: These are some of the tools to get you to "no mind." This is where your real power lies. This is where you grow, vertically. Gain depth. This is the place of true creativity.

We're all artists creating our lives. That is how much power you really have.

Take it. Own it. Live it!

THE VINEYARD

When I was a boy growing up on our farm in the Yakima Valley, I was surrounded by vineyards and rows of asparagus. They were some of my favorite memories of my childhood. My family, come harvest time, would either harvest the field ourselves, or we would hire pickers and cutters.

Oh, asparagus. The smell of fresh-cut asparagus. It still brings me memories.

I never got to harvest the asparagus plants. But I got to smell their earthy, green scent while riding in the big green GMC truck my grandfather drove to town each morning to process his crop.

Memories. How they seem so far away. Yet a distinct scent, a thought, can bring them so near. It was beautiful to experience growing up on the farm, almost like a fairytale to me now.

The grapes in early October, I recall the clearest. The sweet smell of fully ripe grapes in the hot air of an afternoon. A fragrance the family expected and waited for all summer long while I was growing up.

The grape leaves turning colorful fall hues after the harvest, adding to the beautiful scenery of our farm amongst the rolling hills. And looking west...Mount Adams to the left, majestic Mount Rainier to the right. And the Yakima River on the horizon.

The vibrant scenery's still there. However, the vineyards when I visit now are all gone. The asparagus is even more moons in the past.

Even today, when I sit silently and think back to life on the farm, I can still smell the sweetness of our grapes. Of golden leaves torn loose and flapping when the fall winds would come down from the mountains.

The farm taught me many lessons. It taught me the beauty of commitment. Of carefully planting seeds. Of caring for them daily. Of watering these little plants yearly till one day they each gave fruit. Fruit in abundance.

After the harvest, it gave even greater beauty. Leaves of orange and red. Leaves of gold. Oh, that sight. The plant. It never held back, even after we took its bounty. It kept on giving, sometimes for years on end.

Our vineyards weren't three years old; they weren't ten years old. They were over forty years old. They gave endlessly till the day they were finally gone.

Their best "fruit," I see now, was the lesson that it isn't at our apex that we reach true beauty, It isn't at total maturity. Our true beauty can also exist in the decline. The graceful decline.

Then...then...I recall the artistry in my seventy-year-old dad and in my ninety-three-year-old grandmother. My older uncles, my aunts. The smiles in their eyes, still full of youth. Still connected to the true meaning of family.

The beauty of commitment. The power of togetherness.

STORIES, MYTHS, FAIRYTALES, AND DREAMS

We love myths. We love stories. Especially those with deep meanings. For, in essence, we are those stories. Our entire society, our entire humanity lives these stories every day.

Joseph Campbell, the great mythologist, studied stories his entire life from all types of religions and tribes—Native American, Hindu, Buddhist, Christian. He believed that stories sustain our society. He concluded that the stories and myths often held the same meaning for different cultures that produced them. The same parable would be told across millennia in different languages and would contain the same archetypes. The same threads of wisdom.

How in the world did that happen? We think that in today's modern society, we have escaped the great Greek myths, that the Hopi stories of old don't have anything to do with us. Yet that's not really true. We're still a tribe, and just like ancient ones, we're still all searching for life's meaning.

I personally have felt the utmost elation and hope while reading stories and poems hundreds of years old. I wouldn't have made it to this point without their metaphors that speak to me on a personal level. I can see why these stories continue to be told today.

I once read that the language of the soul speaks in metaphors and longer allegories. If we read past the words and consider these stories using the language of the soul, we will see their metaphorical truth. These stories, these myths, and even philosophical Hollywood movies often have the same underlying message, much like that of the Hero's Journey (which is the archetype that Campbell mentions in his book *The Hero with a Thousand Faces*).

We could use the Hero's Journey story as a metaphor for our own personal transformation. In the book, Campbell mentions that at times, our life journey can call for an adventure in which we must traverse the unknown. If we apply this to ourselves, we could say that our soul yearns for its release, its freedom. And by taking a step into this new adventure, you face your personal fears head-on and slay the dragons or dark forces—maybe the ego—that has been holding you back. During this adventure, you may encounter many tests, such as the dark night of the soul, in which you may want to return to your previous path. But it is through these challenging encounters, during which we slowly start to regain our truth, that we rise and enter a new, illuminated white space. Finally, diving into the rapture of the divine, feeling this internal light, finding our way home.

By crossing over your personal threshold from the known limits of your world into the unknown, an internal metamorphosis transforms you, and what emerges is a different you. A you with more awareness, enthusiasm, compassion, and love. With gifts that, upon your return, you can bestow on the world.

The main theme of the greatest timeless stories is transformation, with the hero being the one who changes the most. According to Campbell, this common thread also resides in the stories of Gautama Buddha, Moses, and Jesus.

Essentially, a spiritual journey is something common to all of us. We are all the same, and we all want the same things. We all just want to find our way home. We are born in magnificence, in a world of love. A world of awe, wonder, and beauty. Then slowly, we stumbled out of connection. This is our mostly inescapable human condition.

Unless we one day realize that there is a way out. And it's the soul. If you develop the courage to follow it, your soul will lead you back home. Back to the world within worlds. To the light. The place that Jesus, Buddha, and all the great ones mentioned.

Despite humanity's larger story, it's your own personal story that really matters. The one you are currently writing and live every day. The story you write one word at a time, say one word at a time, turn into one action one moment at a time.

You are a storyteller. Yes, indeed you are. You are writing a so-called myth for generations yet to be born. You are a creator, first and foremost. The hero of your own journey.

The individual stories we write every day are all intricately connected across space and time. We are all indeed master storytellers and writers weaving a magnificent story. And we have time...yes, we do, to write the greatest shared story ever told.

May the beauty of a story, a fairytale, a myth, or a dream light the ember that lies deep within you. And let it burn. Let it burn!

THE UNENDING WELL OF LOVE

If you've ever been betrayed or had the experience of feeling unappreciated, you've likely asked, "Why should we give—and continue to give—if people don't acknowledge or aren't grateful for us sharing a bit of ourselves?"

Once upon a time, we gave and gave with complete abandon, with total innocence. We didn't care as kids what people thought of us. We just wanted to share. Maybe it was something small, or maybe we shared something big, at least, big to us. And maybe one day someone turned our giving into something painful and bewildering. They took our gift and crumpled it like paper. They threw it back at us. They took our love and burned it down.

Everyone on this planet has tasted that feeling. That total destruction of a gift they gave. So, most of us learn over time to hold back.

It's like a faucet of running water. The water was our flowing gift. Then someone took the faucet knob and turned it off. And so, we stopped giving.

Yet who are they to do that? Who are they to take

our gift and shut it down? This game of life is about us. Our task in this game is to keep the flow going. It's seeing someone reach for that faucet knob and grabbing their hand and saying: "No! Not today!"

Maybe you don't like the way my water flows...maybe you don't like what my gift involves. But let's be clear on this. The water must flow. For it's life.

Whether my form of flowing gift agrees with you is not my concern. I respect your opinion. However, you do not have the power to block this flow.

For it is you who holds that power. It is you who can start and stop the flow. So, keep the water flowing...keep giving. Keep on moving forward. Turn the knob back on and let the water flow. Let the level of the water rise.

Keep rising to a higher level of giving. Until one day, you will meet people at your level. Or maybe they will find you. These people will say, "Yes! That is the level we like. That is the level where we live."

And you'll all just smile...and laugh. For the water flows, and it builds. It rises up to higher levels of consciousness, where a new type of world begins. It's a world of acceptance. A world of beauty...

The water, of course, is love. And it comes from an unending well.

ONENESS

In this world of many possible perceptions, it can be hard to discover the full beauty of who you really are. To connect to the beauty that permits full appreciation of this ride we call life. Most of us think that everyone sees reality the same as we do. However, if we dig a little deeper, we begin to understand that our world is completely different than everyone else's.

Life expresses itself through many avenues. Some call these avenues different expressions of consciousness. Each of us is a unique being. Life will never see, feel, or hear the world in the same way that you do ever again. The uniqueness of your experience is yours and yours alone.

These differences only exist, though, because of different perceptions. For here lies a great paradox: Even though we all see and live in different conceptual worlds, at our core, we are all the same.

It is from that deep insight that you break open to a truer understanding. In understanding our interconnectedness, you will start to know yourself...as well as others.

Through this process of self-understanding, we all start to build empathy and compassion, not only for others but ourselves as well.

The greatest secret ever told was that we are indeed all. One. To realize this may be your greatest accomplishment, for it breaks you free of a life of duality, the good and the bad, the highs and the lows, the negatives and the positives, and the joys and the fear.

To realize this for oneself is to realize that you are at One with existence. That everything you see, including yourself, is consciousness on different levels, and it is indeed coming from the same source: life. This is the true meaning of Oneness. You're a point of consciousness, a wave on the surface of the ocean of life.

It has taken eons for us to get to this point of human evolution. For life to recognize itself for what it is. We are all inseparable from each other. We are life being expressed in millions of myriad ways. We are home. You are home. Right now, in this moment. In the eternity of this moment.

It is diving into this moment and embracing what is in front of us that will change our individual worlds. In doing so, you will actually change the entire world. For you are the entire world. In understanding this lies the greatness of your own personal power.

Spiritual enlightenment is nothing more than realizing that life is who we really are, life recognizing itself amongst its many forms of existence. For the real you is that point of awareness that is silent, that is still, that is anchored, solid, immovable...watching, experiencing it all.

In that self-realization, healthy selves, healthy worlds are born. The cutting edge of life. This knowledge brings an end, finally, to the struggle of fighting others, and thus, fighting ourselves. Finally, the freedom to just be. Finally finding our way home.

LIFE'S LOWS AND PEAKS

Sometimes when you find yourself experiencing a really rough situation in life, you might wonder how or why this came to be. You may ask what you did to deserve this. Sometimes the oasis can seem so far away. Some of us give up, become bitter, walk away from the dream. We may even choose to walk away from what matters in our life.

Yet without the desert, without that little bit of suffering, you will never really taste the sweetest part of life. You might never really understand or enjoy the magnificence of those peak moments. For the highest peaks on this world were cut from deep valleys.

To some, life can seem like a path carved with pain, with bitter sorrow, just a mist amongst the trees. But at times we can see through the fog to a clearing that we ourselves have rediscovered.

As hard as it may seem to see the light amidst the darkness, the darkness is ultimately no match for the light. No match for true life, revealing itself as that light we really are. For there is indeed love when we think there is no more to give.

Up ahead lies more mountains to climb, many more paths to create, many rivers yet to cross.

Much more...yet, to give.

SELF-REALIZATION

It's not an easy thing to fathom, is it? To understand that everything is a part of the whole. Just as a drop of ocean water is made of the same substance as its origin, the sea. Or consider a rock that still contains the same elements as its source, the mountain.

Even though the drop of water and the rock are minuscule descendants, they never lose the elements of their origin. If we look at a microscopic drop of water compared to the sea, we wouldn't be able to tell the difference. Same with the rock. Each small part still echoes the essence of its source. That's where the term "Oneness" comes from.

The mind can have a hard time grasping this concept. Actually, the mind cannot grasp it. But the soul. The soul knows. That's why feelings are your best guide.

That moment of realizing Oneness...is the point that we call enlightenment, cosmic consciousness, self-realization, self-actualization. It really doesn't matter what term we use. It's our evolutionary goal.

So, is it a mystical moment? Oh, yes, I do believe so.

For when it happens, your world will stop. Time will stop. And you'll come to know that, yes...you are part of the stars. That, yes...you are a mystical part of everything that ever came before you. And that you will be a part of whatever comes after.

There really is no death. Because energy can never disappear. It just transforms. It moves. It evolves to the point where it, where you, come to understand that, yes...

We...
Are all...indeed...,
One.

THE ROSE

The rose. She spoke to me of feelings she had,
of petals that she had lost.
While in bloom, she told me, "I lost a few petals,
Petals of beauty that came from the essence of my core."

"But as I continued to bloom underneath
this morning's sun,
some were lost. Lost to the wind. Lost to beauty.
They delicately floated back to the ground."

She then whispered me a story...a secret, really.
That those petals lost to the earth were never really lost.
Over time, they fertilized her. They gave her more life.

She went on to say..."My petals never completely vanish.
It is all an illusion. The petal deteriorates, yes, and
becomes part of the soil.
However, the secret is these petals made it
more inviting for me to keep blooming.
For me to keep flowering. Year after year, petal
after long-lost petal.
For indeed they've never gone anywhere.
They are right here.

Right in front of your eyes. The beauty you see
is all of them, really.
Keep looking, for my rosebud holds potential
Of everything that was, and for everything that will be.

It holds You. It holds Me.

For the highest magnificence is the fragrance
that all my petals give together.
A symphony, really. A melody. A song of life.
Of a game we all choose to play. Of love, really.
Touch it lightly. Feel its splendor.
Don't play coy with me! Come dance the dance
you seek and bloom with me.
To the radiance of the sun, which feeds us.
The rain that grows us."

Give. Give, young petal, of everything you have.
For it will never go unnoticed.
It will only feed my bloom. My alluring fragrance.

And it will do so in time, my friend...it will, in time.
For everything has its season.
Everything is just fine.

— Roman

THE STORY OF US ALL

I was born a dreamer
Always have been
Yet maybe someday, my dreams will somehow catch up
to me
Someday
Maybe
They will become my life.

A writer
That's what I am
A whisperer of stories
Of sayings
A pleasure in words
Of worlds not yet seen.
And I love it all!

A harmonious experience
Words written and words not yet written
Of a life done
And not yet done.

A creator of the greatest story ever told
And that is the story of my life:

Lived
Not written.

Nothing having been wasted
Nothing having been done in vain

The life of a real writer, a real storyteller
The experience if it all

That's who we all are.

— Roman

AFTERWORD

I've learned for the most part now to keep my mouth shut, to just smile, to float in the water and bob with the waves. Maybe it's my age now. Maybe it's finally some wisdom kicking in.

But it's comforting, I tell you, to let the water's warmth cover you. For it will give you the ability to float on top. Oh, yes! The water may splash you in unexpected ways. And I sometimes decide to cling to the banks or try to swim back upstream.

However, over time, I'll remember to give in to it. For it will still let you come up for air. The trick is in not fighting it. The trick is in letting it take you where it wants to take you. For the water's wisdom is beyond words...beyond the mind.

Ultimately, if you let it, it will take you back. Back to the place you wanted to go in the first place. To a little place within yourself, your real, true self. To a little place where you experience bliss. A little place we call love. A place we all call home.

Peace!

— Roman

THE STILLNESS

Out of nothing
Everything is born

Out of the ether
Creativity awaits.

To sit still
Is one of the hardest things we can do

To meditate
To ponder
Can seem so weak.

Yet out of nothing
Comes one of the greatest strengths
We can conceive

For out of nothing comes a breath,
Out of stillness comes life

The edge of stillness,
The birth point of creativity.

As the flower blooms in silence,
So do we.

— Roman

BIBLIOGRAPHY

Bradshaw, John. *Homecoming: Reclaiming and Championing Your Inner Child.* Reprint Edition. New York: Bantam, 1992.

Campbell, Joseph. *The Power of Myth.* With Bill Moyers. New York: Anchor Books, 1991.

Campbell, Joseph. *The Hero with a Thousand Faces (The Collected Works of Joseph Campbell)* 3rd Edition. Novato, CA: New World Library, 2008.

Castaneda, Carlos. *The Active Side of Infinity.* New York: Harper Perennial, 1999.

Chopra, Deepak. *How to Know God: The Soul's Journey into the Mystery of Mysteries.* New York: Harmony, 2001.

Cummings, E.E. *A Miscellany*, rev. ed. George James Firmage. New York: Liveright, 2018.

de Chardin, Pierre Teilhard. *The Divine Milieu*. New York: Harper Perennial Modern Classics, 2001.

Gilbert, Daniel. *Stumbling on Happiness*. New York: Random House, 2006.

Johnson, Richard L. *Ghandi's Experiments with Truth: Essential Writings by and about Mahatma Gandhi (Studies in Comparative Philosophy and Religion)*. Lanham, MD: Lexington Books, 2005.

Juan Mascaró, trans., *The Upanishads*. Later Printing Edition. London: Penguin Classics, 1965.

Keller, Hellen. *The Open Door: A Sense of Life: Selections From the Writings of Helen Keller*. With a foreword by Katharine Cornell. New York: Doubleday & Co., 1957.

Krishnamurti, Jiddu. *The Collected Works of J. Krishnamurti – Volume II 1934-1935: What is Right Action?* Ojai, CA: K Publications, 2012. Content reproduced with permission (see below).

Nelson, Thomas. *The King James Study Bible, Large Print, Hard Cover, Red Letter Edition,* 2nd ed. Nashville: Thomas Nelson, 2013.

Plato. *The Republic*. New Edition. Translated by Desmond Lee. London: Penguin Classics, 2007.

Trine, Ralph Waldo. *In Tune With The Infinite: Or Fullness of Peace, Power, and Plenty*. n.p.: CreateSpace Independent Publishing Platform, 2015.

Underhill, Evelyn. *Practical Mysticism: A Little Book for Normal People and Abba: Meditations Based on the Lord's Prayer*. New York: Vintage, 2003, 1657.

Walsch, Neale Donald. *Communion with God (Conversations with God Series)*. New York: TarcherPerigee, 2002.

Whitman, Walt. *Leaves of Grass: The First (1855) Edition*. Reprint. Edited by Malcolm Cowley. New York: Penguin Classics, 1961.

Acknowledgment: Permission to quote from the works of J. Krishnamurti or other works for which the copyright is held by the Krishnamurti Foundation of America or the Krishnamurti Foundation Trust Ltd has been given on the understanding that such permission does not indicate endorsement of the views expressed in this publication. For more information about J. Krishnamurti (1895–1986), please see: www.jkrishnamurti.org.

ABOUT THE AUTHOR

In *Rowing Home*, Castilleja takes readers from Washington State to Texas as he recaps the highs and lows of rediscovering the spiritual truths that underpin life. Based on years of personal examination since his rowing experience, as well as spontaneous writings that began after reawakening his spiritual connection, Castilleja also provides dozens of accessible meditations about life's biggest mysteries, such as how to animate your soul, harness your ego, and face tragedies.

Born in Sunnyside, Washington, Castilleja shares his prose and poetry about spiritual growth at www.romancastilleja.com. He currently divides his time between the Pacific Northwest and Austin, Texas.